D0277089

# BRAIN MECHANISMS AND MIND

'The sensory messages are scarcely more complex than a succession of dots in the Morse code.'

E. D. Adrian in *The Mechanism of Nervous Action*

'How complex must not the central processes then be in order to explain the workings of our mind.'

Rejoinder attributed to C. S. Sherrington

THE WORLD OF SCIENCE LIBRARY

GENERAL EDITOR: ROBIN CLARKE

# BRAIN MECHANISMS AND MIND

## Keith Oatley

 THAMES AND HUDSON  LONDON

UNIVERSITY LIBRARY

19 AUG 1974

LANCASTER

Any copy of this book issued by the publisher as
a paperback is sold subject to the condition that it
shall not, by way of trade or otherwise, be lent,
resold, hired out or otherwise circulated, without
the publisher's prior consent, in any form of binding
or cover other than that in which it is published, and
without a similar condition including this condition
being imposed on a subsequent purchaser.

All rights reserved. No part of this publication may
be reproduced or transmitted in any form or by any
means, electronic or mechanical, including photocopy,
recording or any information storage and retrieval system,
without permission in writing from the publisher.

© 1972 Keith Oatley

Set by Filmtype Services Limited, Scarborough
Printed in Holland by Smeets Lithographers, Weert
Bound in Holland by Proost en Brandt NV, Amsterdam

0 500 08011 9 Clothbound
0 500 10011 x Paperback

# CONTENTS

# PREFACE

This book is an attempt to introduce, and discuss a view of, a field of research that has as yet no single name to gather it together. It includes neurophysiology, the experimental psychology of animals and men, linguistics and artificial intelligence. It may seem absurd to try and write so small a book on so wide a subject. I would not have done so but for the conviction that the field has unity, and that its coherence needs to be emphasized. Because the book is short, and because I have tried to write about ideas and concepts rather than just facts, the way in which I have discussed various matters may seem biased. I can only invite readers to disagree with me as they see fit, and hope that I have stated arguments sufficiently clearly to allow them to do so.

In calling the book *Brain Mechanisms and Mind* I am aware of philosophical difficulties that surround the term 'mind'. My reasons for using it notwithstanding are that this field is concerned not just with brain physiology or with behaviour but with mental processes as well. The fact that behaviour is perhaps the principal observable datum in this field does not confine us to behaviourism, any more than interest in mental processes obliges us to accept the explanations of mentalism. Nor does use of the term 'brain' imply an exclusive concern for brain tissue. The object of the field of enquiry for which 'brain research' seems a rather inadequate name, is the understanding of the principles and organization that make behaviour and mental processes possible. In using the word 'brain' therefore I simply wish to imply that the mental processes and behaviour of man depend upon a physical organ, and in using the term 'mind' for some of the higher of these processes I do not wish to imply that the brain is the only device in which they could ever be embodied. For instance, some of the work described in this book represents attempts to embody processes normally associated with mind within computers.

I would like to thank those of my friends and my colleagues in the Laboratory of Experimental Psychology at Sussex who by their discussions and research interests have contributed to these ideas. In particular I am grateful to R. B. Boakes, Pearl Goodwin, Sebastian Halliday, John Scholes, Robin Stanton and N. S. Sutherland, who were kind enough to read the manuscript and make critical comments and helpful suggestions. I should like to thank Colin Atherton who gave photographic assistance, Stephen England, Leslie Hay and Malcolm Topp of Thames and Hudson who helped produce the book, Stella Frost and Harriet Matyniak who typed drafts of the manuscript, and also my wife Sally who both typed and commented.

*Keith Oatley*
*University of Sussex 1971*

The task of finding out how the brain works is probably the most difficult that science has faced. We need merely to turn to the evidence of human behaviour to see how complex the problem is, or if that is not enough, to reflect that the human brain contains about ten million million connections between its nerve cells. The challenge of brain research, as it now appears, is to explain how the mental capacities and behaviour of man depend on the patterns of these interconnections.

It may be pointless trying to understand the brain. Its enormous complexity may defeat us. The only means we have for understanding it is our own brain, and perhaps it would take a brain yet more complex to attain such comprehension. Brain research would also be impossible, or at least always depressingly incomplete, if the brain were not in some sense a physical system. Mental processes might interact with the physical brain in some way, but nevertheless be fundamentally non-physical. No amount of argument can prove or disprove this possibility; it is an empirical question. Only if we could ever finally understand mental events and behaviour on the basis of physical principles would the question be settled. For the present, the scientist believes that mental processes are produced by the physical brain, for if they were not, the whole apparatus of science would be inadequate for investigating them.

But these are arguments of pessimism. Let us suppose

*Opposite: the mechanisms of human behaviour and mental function are so complex that it has been almost impossible to know how to start to understand them. The seventeenth-century physician and mystic Robert Fludd thought man's mind was composed of several aspects such as intellect, imagination and sensation, combining in the head to form the mind*

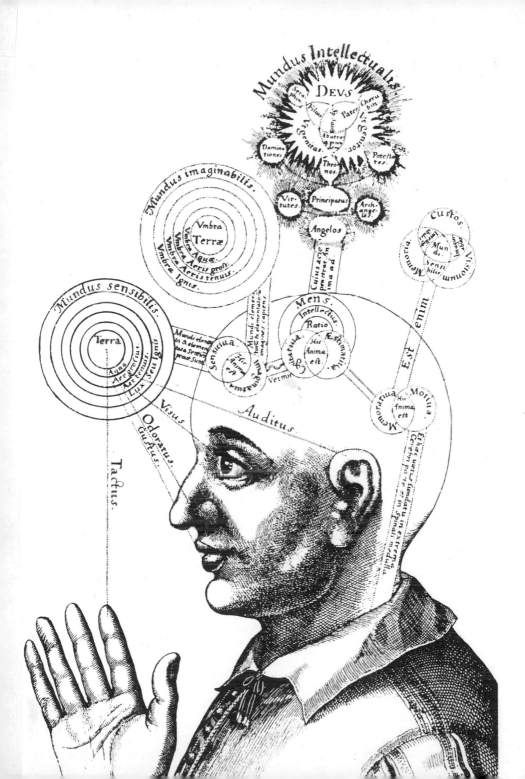

that the scientific study of brain mechanisms and mind is possible and will finally be successful. This book is about some of the understandings reached so far.

## Principles of brain research

The reason why sublime properties of the mind have formerly seemed incompatible with the rather mechanical processes of the body was not that we had too high a conception of mind, but that we had too mean an understanding of the capabilities of mechanism. Machines that pump and propel may have few of the properties associated with mind, but the machines which control and calculate, the computers, have many.

When today we seek to understand the brain in terms of physical processes, we propose mechanisms of an altogether more sophisticated order than were imagined even thirty years ago. Then there was little evidence that physical devices could behave in a way that could be regarded as intelligent. Today computers answer questions, recognize patterns, play intellectual games, and prove mathematical theorems. One quite safe conclusion is that intelligent behaviour of a high order (and in some cases of a higher order than most

*Early attempts to mimic behaviour, such as this 'duck' made in about 1738, embodied no very profound principles*

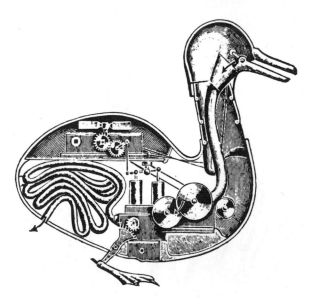

*More modern artificial behaviour such as the computer program of Elcock and Murray which plays Go Moku (a kind of extended noughts and crosses) is much more impressive and can compete on more than equal terms with man. This particular program learns from being beaten and improves its game until human players cannot win*

of us can produce) can be based entirely on a physical device.

Ever since it has been possible to imagine that mind might be understood in terms of the workings of the brain there have been two threads running through brain research. The first is the attempt to understand how mental processes and behaviour might be carried out at all. What kinds of mechanism could conceivably be responsible? What possible principles could be involved? The second, which is dependent upon the first, is, How then are these processes and principles embodied in the networks of nerve cells in the brain?

The reasons why it now seems likely that mind will one day be explained in terms of the workings of a physical brain are, firstly, that we have begun to understand some of the principles that would make mental processes possible. Secondly, neurophysiology has shown that nerve cells, or neurones as they are also called, have the properties and the organization which would allow them to embody these principles of mind within the brain.

## The brain as a model of the world
A prerequisite for understanding anything about the brain is a grasp of what kind of thing it is. Is it fundamentally a piece of machinery that collects sensory

*Kenneth Craik had a formative influence in modern experimental psychology and was one of the first to explore principles common to brains and machines. His tragic death in a road accident in 1945 deprived brain research of a brilliant man*

impressions from the world and reacts to them? Is there within the brain some central intelligence that uses the body to enact its master plan? Is there actually anything complicated to explain at all; do we not see and hear and act in the world because the world out there is what it is? Depending on our view, our approach to finding out how the brain works will obviously be affected. Furthermore, until each possible approach has been tried, argued about, and experimented upon, it is not easy to see how adequate it may be.

How then should we view the brain? One fruitful idea is that the brain is a complex information-processing device that contains an internal model of the outside world. Why the brain needs to represent internally the events and processes of the world in order to be responsible for behaviour is part of the subject of this book.

This notion seems first to have been put with force and clarity in the context of brain research by Kenneth Craik in 1943. Craik was only thirty-one when he was knocked off his bicycle, by someone carelessly opening a car door, and run over. Though Craik's research life was short, his influence has been profound. He proposed that mental processes represent within the brain the nature of the outside world. The brain, in other words, acts as a model in which neural processes symbolize the workings of the external world and thus allow us to predict the outcome of events and of our own actions. When I say, 'I must leave now if I am to catch the train', the form of words presupposes mental structures (with neural processes underlying them) which represent time, the speed at which I can travel towards the station, its direction, distance and so forth. These mental structures mirror, in a symbolic form, objects and their inter-relationships. If mental processes did not accurately represent important features of the real world, we could never catch the train; nor indeed would trains ever have been built. Only occasionally would random behaviour ever bring about a favourable outcome.

Since the brain-model represents the kinds of events that can occur in the world, we can try out 'what would happen if', without the usually useless and occasionally dire consequences of actually doing it. This vicarious nature of thought seems to be a key to many higher mental processes, but the necessity of a model to represent the world is no less important for mundane matters. If I wanted to make a cup of coffee, how would I know how to do so without some sort of plan of how to get to the kitchen and perform the necessary actions? What else would such a plan be but a set of mental operations organized around some representation or model of the layout of the house and the properties of gas stoves, kettles and teaspoons?

'Why', it may be asked, 'is all this talk of representation necessary? Is there not a perfectly good external world already there towards which we can direct our behaviour, without making models of it?' The answer is that without a means for creating a model world with similar properties to those of the real one, but nevertheless independent of it, thought, language, perception, purposive action and a number of other attributes of the mind are (so far as we can see) impossible.

One of the grand ideas of biology is that to be able to live an existence free of a constant and sustaining sea, animals evolved to carry around inside them their own private sea; the blood and other fluids that surround the cells of the body. Claude Bernard pointed out that by maintaining this internal environment constant and well stocked with nutrients, animals can live a free life although the external environment is capricious and hostile. The idea of a model of the world within the brain has some similar features. The model enables the brain to be to some extent independent of the actual world, but free to move about within it.

Without such a concept we would be stuck with exactly the kind of billiard-ball determinism that those who argue against a physical basis for mind quite rightly insist is insufficient. With only the world out

*Paramecia are single-celled animals which simply react to the stimuli that impinge on them. On encountering an obstacle or unpleasant substance – such as the alkaline solution in the centre of this time-lapse photograph – several of the paramecia (seen as blobs at the front of long tails marking their recent tracks) have turned away*

there to guide behaviour we could react to stimuli, but never predict the outcome of any action. We could never direct behaviour to anything beyond the immediate range of sense organs; never behave purposefully since that implies the imagination of a state of the world that does not yet exist. We could never create, but only respond.

## Thought

Craik's view of the nature of thought was that it consists of three stages. First, information from sense organs must be translated into neural and mental symbolism, representing objects and events in the world. Then these internal symbols must be manipulated within the model according to rules which mirror the workings of the world. Finally there must either be a retranslation of these derived symbols into behaviour that can affect the world, or at least recognition of their relation to external events.

The business of making models is quite a familiar

process. A map models an area of land by representing real objects as symbolic ink marks whose relative distances and directions from each other on the map represent spatial relationships of real objects on the ground. In finding our own way about in the world it seems necessary to represent mentally the same kind of spatial relationships between objects.

Working models extend this idea. The device invented by Kelvin to predict the tides symbolizes the height of water by the distance of a pulley from a line, and represents the cyclically changing forces

*Kelvin's tidal predictor: a working model which represents important aspects of astronomical influences on seas and allows times and heights of tides to be forecast*

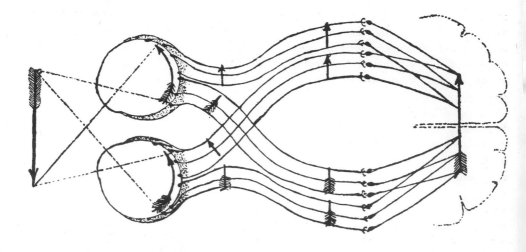

*A sketch from Ramon y Cajal's famous book on the histology of the nervous system, showing how the spatial relationships of an image on the retina are retained in the arrangement of cells that are stimulated in the visual cortex at the back of the brain. However, maintenance of spatial relationships does not constitute recognition*

acting on the oceans (due to the rotation of the earth, the rotation round it of the moon, and so on) by other pulleys moving periodically up and down. The model symbolizes the real behaviour of the tides, and in this case it is able to do so because such things as distance and periodic motion are universal, and are exhibited by many different arrangements of objects.

This does not mean that if in the brain spatial relationships are modelled, directions and scaled-down distances within the brain represent them. Indeed symbolizing the dimensions of space as a scaled-down space between nerve cells would serve no purpose in this context, because what we know about nerve cells indicates that they do not operate in terms of distances or directions. Instead they translate such attributes into symbolic codes upon which logical operations are performed by networks of neurones. A system of logical operations has a power and versatility of symbolism that is quite unmatched. Although in detail the mechanisms of computers and brains are very different, logical operations also provide the basis for the computer's considerable abilities.

Mathematics is an example of a structure of logical symbolism. There needs to be nothing sevenish about the symbol 7 in order for it to represent an aspect of the real world. What is necessary is that the logical system within which it operates is self consistent, maintains correspondence between certain stages of the symbolic process and what is represented, and allows translation back and forth between symbolism and reality.

## Models and theories

We use symbolic mental processes of language and arithmetic all the time. Scale models, differential equations, computers and so on can also be used to supplement our internal symbolism, since these external models may exhibit important aspects of a process more clearly than the real process itself, and our own logical capacity may be too feeble. In scientific explanation as well, a theory is a model of the processes which it is to explain, and the truth of a theory is tested by the correspondence of its predictions with reality.

In recent years the digital computer has come to be used as the device which can *par excellence* model or simulate every kind of physical process, and it can do so with the same order of flexibility as the brain itself. The computer, therefore, is a tool which can help us to understand our own brain, for only in the computer do we have a device of sufficient complexity or versatility to hold a theory (or model) of the brain. In trying to program computers to behave in the way that brains do, moreover, we have to include in the program means by which the computer too can represent the world. The computer, like the brain, must be able to model the world if a computer program is to be an adequate theory of brain processes.

None of this emphasis on models implies that the brain merely represents the outside world, and that that is all there is to it. The concept of a model mainly concerns what knowledge about the nature of the world is embodied in the brain, and how that knowledge is arranged and organized. It does not necessarily concern the business of how the processes of the brain are guided in purposeful directions, nor of how symbols are interpreted. As Craik made clear, the outcome of mental activity is recognition of the significance of the products of thought, and/or re-translation of the mental symbolism back into actions which affect the outside world.

The processes of modelling, directing and interpreting are therefore central to the brain. The task is to find out how they are done. In order to do this we must study the brain at many different levels. It is no good merely studying nerve cells. We would never be able to understand how a computer played chess simply by studying its transistors and pieces of wire. We must therefore investigate not only the brain, but also behaviour, and not only the human brain and behaviour, but also those of animals and even the computers which we ourselves have invented and programmed.

Correspondingly, our explanations will need to be at many different levels. At a lower level understanding will involve specification of how nerve cells with particular properties are connected so that they perform given functions. But higher-level functions will depend on these, and brain mechanisms at higher

*Imagine we were trying to find out how a computer worked. Below right is a plan of the circuit layout of a minute memory chip; below is a diagram of a single logic circuit. No amount of analysis of the computer at these levels would alone allow us to understand how it performed any kind of complex behaviour. We need also to understand principles underlying behaviour at many different levels, including the kind embodied in the flow diagram opposite, which might form the basis of a computer program to play second (X) at noughts and crosses (tic tac toe). As a matter of fact a program based on this scheme could be beaten; try playing against it*

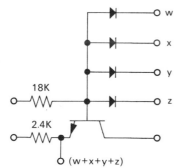

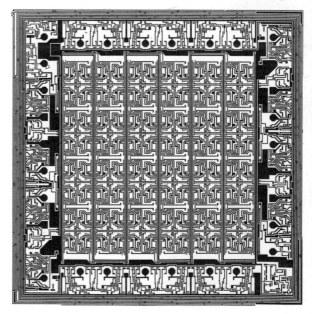

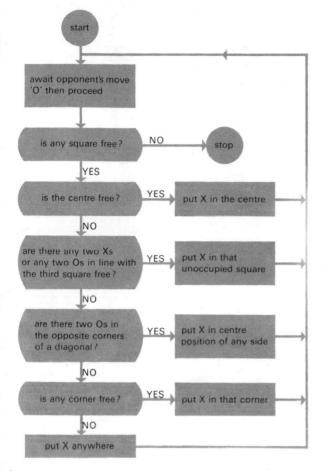

levels can still sensibly be called brain mechanisms, although our explanations of them are couched in terms that do not mention nerve cells, but take operations at lower levels for granted.

Ultimately we hope to be able to specify all the important operations involved in mental processes with sufficient rigour to be able to reproduce them in a physical device such as a computer. If this turns out to be possible then we would not need to look further than the physical nature of the brain to explain the workings of mind.

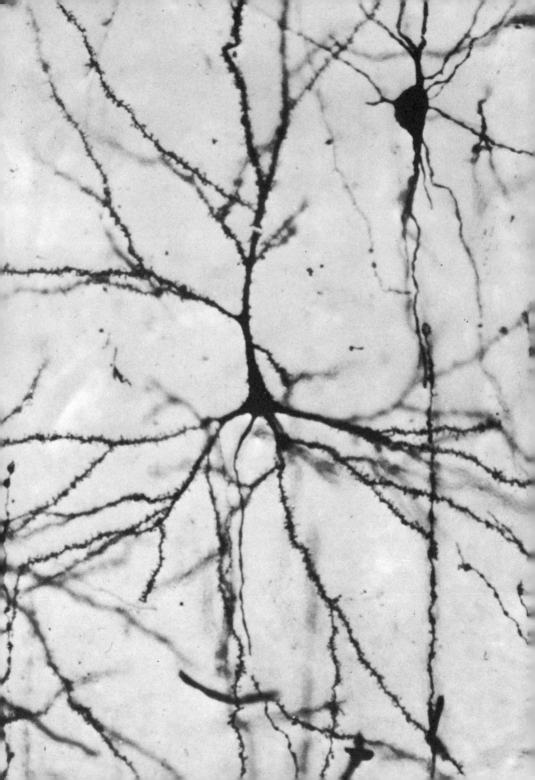

# NEURONES

Though the properties of nerve cells do not, as such, explain how the brain works, these properties must be understood to see how cells can be interconnected to provide a basis for brain mechanisms.

A neurone has a structure fitted to its two main functions of transmitting information over long distances and of collecting together information so that messages arriving from different sources or at different times can interact to allow logical operations and computation.

The part of the nerve cell used for transmission of information, the axon, is rather thin, ranging in mammals from about half a micron (a micron is one millionth of a metre) in diameter to about twenty microns. Although axons branch repeatedly, a single neurone has only one axon transmitting signals *away* from the body cell. The rest of the cell, comprising the cell body and the dendrites, has a surface that collects information from other neurones. Dendrites are elongated continuations of the cell body. Unlike the axon their diameter narrows as they extend from the cell body.

Some idea of the neurone's shape and proportions can be grasped by imagining a single neurone from the brain enlarged by a factor of 10,000. On this scale the cell body would be an irregular bulbous object about the size of a football, with dendrites extending to the corners of a small room, in much the same way as would the branches of a small tree. The axon would

*Opposite: a silver-stained neurone from the cortex of the brain. The cell body (in centre of picture) is pyramid shaped, and the dendrites, bearing small knobbly projections which correspond to the positions of synapses, extend from it. The axon is seen as a thin thread running downwards. A nerve cell of another type is seen at the top right*

be a long tube about the diameter of an arm, extending for a distance that might be from 10 to 100 yards within the brain. On the same scale an axon to a muscle or from a sense organ might extend for a mile or more.

Communication between nerve cells takes place at specialized sites known as synapses. Most axons branch profusely before reaching other cells, and at the end of every branch is a synapse. Synapses occur on the surface of the neurone body, and even more profusely on the dendrites, which receive about 80 per cent of all axon terminals.

Neurones can act as switches or logical decision units directing the flow of information. Depending upon the pattern of signals arriving at its synapses, a neurone either does or does not send new signals along its axon. Thus in principle the brain can be thought of as a network of richly interconnected decision-making elements.

These principles of neural organization are not very different from the principles upon which a computer works. Here, too, simple elements capable of acting as switches and logical decision points have rich patterns of interconnection determined by the computer program. The fact that intelligent behaviour can be produced by computers indicates that our own behaviour could also be based upon richly interconnected elements, each of which merely performs simple logical operations.

Each of the fifty thousand million ($5 \times 10^{10}$) neurones in the brain may have a thousand or so synapses upon it, and some cells in the cortex have as many as 60,000. A single switch in a computer, capable of being in one of two states and thus taking a single binary decision, is certainly not analogous in any exact sense to a single neurone. However, some idea of the complexity of the brain can be gained by reflecting that even if a neurone were as simple as a computer binary element, then on the basis of the number of such units, a single human brain would be equivalent to something like a thousand of the larger kind of computers

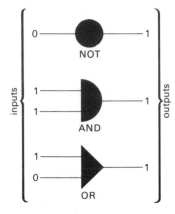

The immense powers of the computer to simulate and calculate depend on elementary logical operations. Simple electronic circuits (such as those illustrated on page 18) can be constructed to give a signal out (1) when no input signal (0) exists, or vice versa (a logical NOT circuit), an output when all inputs are activated (AND), or an output when any input is activated (OR). Neurones do not work in exactly this way, but they too are capable of similar elementary logical operations

Opposite: the cell body of a neurone stained to show the synaptic terminals of axons upon it. One terminal is arrowed

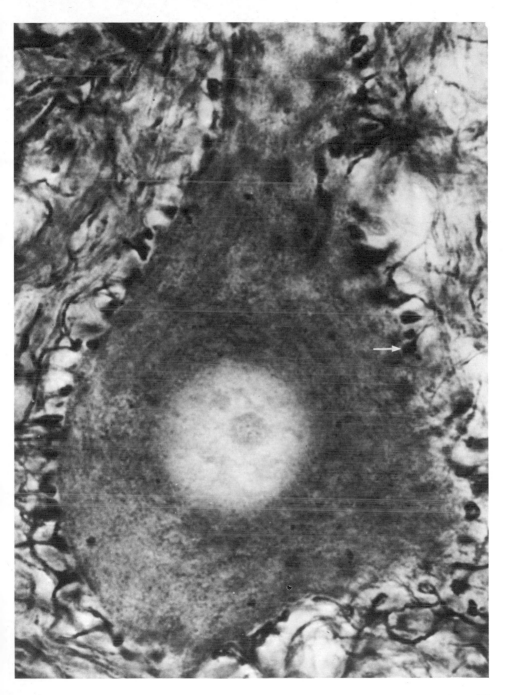

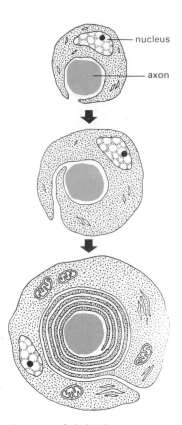

nucleus

axon

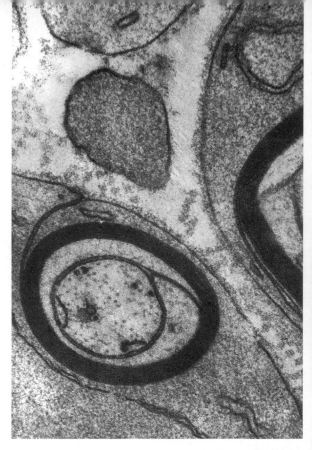

*One type of glial cell acts so as to increase the speed of nerve impulses, wrapping itself round the axon (above) during the development of the nervous system. The spiral layers of myelin can be seen in electron micrographs of axons (right)*

commonly in use at present. If a synapse were thought of as being equivalent to a computer element than the comparison is even more unflattering to computers.

## Glial cells

Many axons, particularly those that run in long tracts or nerve bundles, are surrounded by an insulating material called myelin. It is formed from cells which during development wrap themselves round and round the axon, leaving their own cell membranes behind them to form a spiral white tube of many layers. The whiteness of the myelin stands out from the greyness of cell bodies, and bundles of myelinated axons can be seen running from place to place in the brain, as well as from the brain to the muscles and from sense organs to the brain.

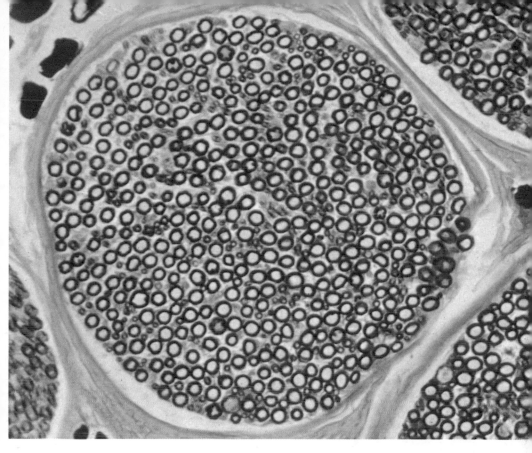

The cells that form the myelin are a type of glial cell. Glia literally means glue, and these cells have been thought to provide a sort of filling for the gaps between nerve cells.

The myelin sheath increases the speed of nerve impulses along axons, and so this accounts for the presence of at least one type of glial cell. The great majority of glia are not of this type however, and glial cells outnumber neurones perhaps by as many as five or ten to one. They do not seem to take part actively in the conduction of nerve impulses and their presence remains puzzling. There is some evidence that their biochemical activities are complementary to those of neurones. Suggestions have even been made that glia hand out instructions which nerve cells obey. Whatever this may mean we have almost no informa-

*A single nerve is composed of many axon fibres which run together to some part of the body. Here they are shown stained black, though unstained the myelin is white and shiny*

*A scene from the Abbé Nollet's book of 1746. In one of Nollet's demonstrations he suspended a boy from silk ropes and electrified him. Small pith balls (seen on the round table) were then attracted towards the boy's hand*

tion about it, whereas the properties of nerve cells do seem to be adequate to provide a basis for the mental processes we wish to explain.

## Nerve impulses

The first clues as to how nerves worked came in the second part of the eighteenth century, a period of intense experimentation with electricity. Electrostatic machines, working from the friction of revolving globes or discs of sulphur or glass, provided the most common artificial source. Electricity was also collected from the atmosphere by aerials equivalent to lightning conductors, and even from electric fishes. During this period there were many experiments in which electricity was applied to living tissues. Doctors (and quacks) electrically stimulated the muscles of paralysed people, producing movement in otherwise motionless limbs, and amazement in the onlookers. One popular demonstration involved electrifying a boy suspended between an electrostatic machine and a few balls of light pith. One can easily perform an experiment which is similar in principle, if not in eccentricity. An object such as a comb or ball-pen can easily be electrified by rubbing it on a dry cloth. It will then attract tiny pieces of paper.

By no means the earliest, but the most famous of these electrical experiments were those of Luigi Galvani in Bologna during the 1780's. He found that frogs' legs twitched when hung on brass hooks from iron railings. He was trying to take advantage of atmospheric electricity to stimulate the frogs' legs, but noticed that twitching could take place even when there was no possibility of atmospheric electricity in the vicinity. So after taking his experiments indoors, and repeating the observations with pairs of wires made of various metals he concluded that the electricity must come from the frog, just as it was known to be produced by electric fish. The metals, he supposed, merely acted as conductors.

Stimulated by this discovery, however, Alessandro Volta invented the first battery. Its essential constituents were two dissimilar metals (positive and negative

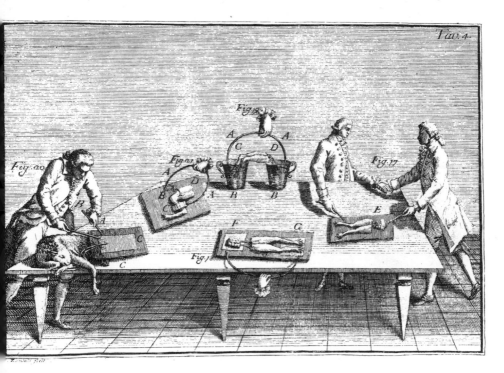

plates of the battery), and a conducting medium between them. Volta argued that the iron and brass in
Galvani's experiments produced the electricity that had
stimulated the frogs' legs, and that the twitches were
merely indicators of the electrical currents flowing.

In the event, Volta turned out to be right, though
this is not to say that electricity is not produced by the
nerves and muscles of animals. It certainly is, though
the amounts are small. Nerves and muscles both produce and respond to electricity; electrical signals are
the means of communication in the nervous system.
Although Galvani was wrong in supposing that his
frogs' legs twitched because of intrinsic electrical
currents, the natural muscular contractions seen when
frogs move their own legs are initiated by electrical
signals. Galvani's experiment with the legs on the
railings worked because a source of electricity was
accidentally created which mimicked the natural
electric currents that provoke movement.

*Luigi Galvani devised many experi-
ments to prove the existence of
'animal electricity', finally con-
cluding that the electricity was contained in a fluid which flowed from
the brain through the nerves to the
muscles. The text of his book
relates how animal preparations were
laid on metal plates, or the spinal
cord was wrapped in lead foil, and
metal arcs used to make circuits
between nerves and muscles. It was
Galvani's most serious critic, Volta,
who realized the significance of the
dissimilar metals in these experiments*

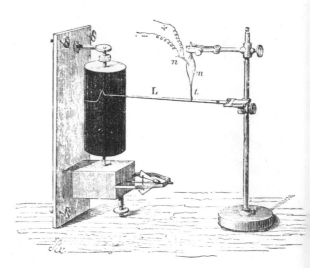

*Hermann von Helmholtz, perhaps the most important figure in brain research. Much of our present understanding of auditory and visual perception is due to his investigations in neurophysiology and experimental psychology. For his measurement of the speed of nerve signals, he developed the myograph (right), seen here as an illustration from the work of an almost equally illustrious colleague, Emil du Bois Reymond. The sciatic nerve (n) can be stimulated electrically and the muscle twitch is traced out on the revolving smoked drum*

In the nineteenth century a succession of notable German physiologists from the laboratory of Johannes Muller elaborated and refined the notion that the nervous system transmitted electrical messages. The most famous of these, Hermann von Helmholtz, with very simple apparatus showed that though the nerve messages were electrical, they did not travel at the speed of electricity along a wire as was thought, but at a very much slower velocity which in the frog was between 90 and 100 feet per second (over 60 miles per hour).

The coming of electronic instruments in the early part of this century produced a number of advances. The 'all-or-nothing' principle of nervous transmission was established: that in a single axon (or nerve fibre) an impulse (the basic unit of a message in an axon) is always the same size and shape. If a nerve is stimulated either all of the impulse occurs, or if the stimulus is not strong enough to reach a certain level (the threshold) then nothing occurs. In other words the nerve impulse is stereotyped, and quite unrelated to the size or type of the stimulating event. The electrical changes of which the impulse consists then trigger the same phenomenon in the adjacent piece of axon, so that the impulse travels steadily and unchangingly along, rather in the same way, but faster, that a small fire travels steadily along a cigarette. Unlike the case of a cigarette though, when the nerve impulse has passed a particular place the source of energy that supported it has not been totally used up. After a delay of about one millisecond (a thousandth of a second) or a little longer, the axon is in a state of readiness for the next impulse.

## The ionic theory of impulse propagation

A cornerstone of our present knowledge of the workings of nerve cells was placed in 1939, when A. L. Hodgkin and A. F. Huxley announced that they had succeeded in recording electrical changes from inside a nerve fibre. Simultaneously and independently the Americans H. J. Curtis and K. F. Cole had been working on the same problem, and their paper appeared in the following year. It is no accident that both English and American groups were working in marine biology laboratories, one in Plymouth, the other at Woods Hole, Massachusetts, because the first recordings from inside a nerve were made in squids.

The luxuriant variation of nature often provides examples of structures which are convenient to experiment upon because of unusual size or accessibility, but which still depend upon the same underlying properties as less convenient if more common specimens. In this case the convenient structure was the squid's giant axon. These nerve fibres, discovered by J. Z. Young in 1933, initiate powerful contractions of the mantle cavity, expelling water and providing the jet propulsion that enables the squid to swim. Young did not fail to point out that these axons, which were up to a millimetre in diameter, might be useful to neurophysiologists.

The recordings that were made in the giant fibres, by inserting a long thin glass capillary electrode into the fluid-filled interior of an axon, revealed a voltage swinging through about a tenth of a volt and lasting about a millisecond as the impulse passed.

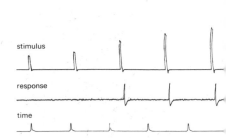

*Above: all-or-nothing activity in the axon. In the top trace electrical stimuli of increasing size are applied; only if they reach the threshold level is a nerve impulse triggered (middle trace) and when this occurs the impulse is always the same. The time marks of the bottom trace are 25 msec apart. One quite apt analogy for the movement of an impulse along an axon is dominoes pushing each other over (below)*

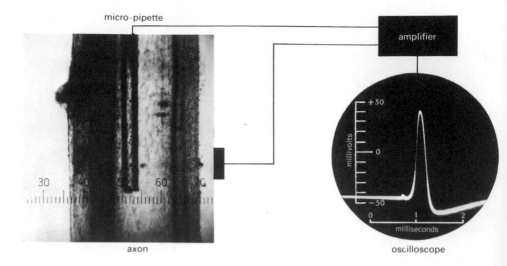

micro-pipette

amplifier

+50

millivolts

0

−50

0    1    2

milliseconds

30    40    50    60    70

axon

oscilloscope

*An electrode inserted into a squid axon (left) by Hodgkin and Huxley allowed the first recordings of the electrical changes across the nerve membrane (right) to be made. The nerve impulse recorded here started from a resting level of −45mV. The resting level depends on a number of factors including the species of animal used and is often larger than this*

The voltage between the inside of the axon and the outside is maintained at a resting level of about minus 60 millivolts (thousandths of a volt) principally by a biochemical mechanism called the 'sodium pump', which acts as a battery charger. Hodgkin and Huxley's experiment confirmed some earlier speculations about the nature of the nerve impulse, but unexpectedly also showed that this resting voltage did not simply collapse with the passage of the impulse, but actually reversed, by going from about 60 millivolts negative to about 40 millivolts positive. Hodgkin, Huxley and other biophysicists have subsequently built upon this important observation to work out the mechanism of nervous conduction in great detail.

The electrical activity of nerves depends upon the electrically charged particles (ions) which exist in the fluids inside and around all the body's cells, including neurones, and a flow of these electrically charged ions constitutes an electric current. Essentially the impulse consists first of the nerve membrane becoming permeable to the electrically positive sodium ions (which are concentrated outside cells by the sodium pump). The increased permeability allows these ions to pass and a few of them rush into the cell, making the inside electrically more positive. But as this is happening there occurs a slightly slower change in permeability to another positively charged ion (potassium) which is concentrated mainly within cells. As potassium ions leave, the inside voltage becomes more negative again, and finally returns to the resting level.

The impulse process works because the changes of permeability in the membrane depend upon the voltage across the membrane. When a nerve fibre is stimulated electrically, either as in Galvani's iron railing experiment or with more sophisticated equipment, an effective stimulus is one that decreases the minus 60 millivolt difference between the inside and outside of the membrane. If that voltage is reduced to about minus 50 millivolts, the threshold level, then the

*The main stages in the generation of the nerve impulse. 1: the membrane becomes selectively permeable to positively-charged sodium ions ($Na^+$) which tend to enter the axon from outside, making the inside potential more positive. Slightly later (2) the membrane becomes permeable to potassium ions ($K^+$) whereupon the voltage returns towards the resting level. The ions have been drawn with different shapes to indicate that a particular pore only passes one type of ion. How this selection occurs is unknown*

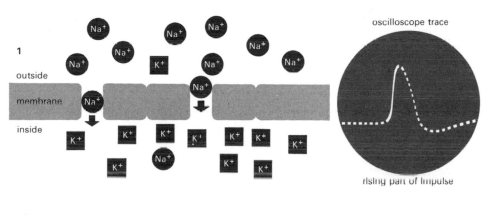

rising part of impulse

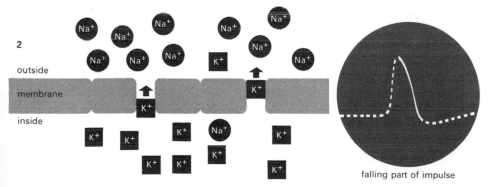

falling part of impulse

membrane starts to become permeable to sodium. As sodium moves into the cell it further decreases the inside negativity of the voltage, which further increases the sodium permeability and hence the inflow of positive sodium ions, forcing the inside voltage more and more in the positive direction. This self-regenerative mechanism in which the sodium permeability increases more and more until the membrane voltage reaches the maximum that can be produced by the sodium concentration, is responsible for the stereotyped all-or-nothing nature of the impulse.

As well as this self-regenerating process, nerve membranes have another property which allows the impulse to travel along. The ion currents spread out passively from the region of the impulse to change the voltage of the membrane ahead, and thus initiate the regenerative activity there.

The speed with which the impulse travels depends upon the ease with which the ion currents can generate the process in adjacent parts of the membrane, and

*The nerve impulse sets up local currents of ion flow which alter the voltage of the membrane ahead of the impulse and trigger the phenomenon there. These currents do not activate the axon in the wake of the impulse because during the recovery phase that section of nerve is insensitive*

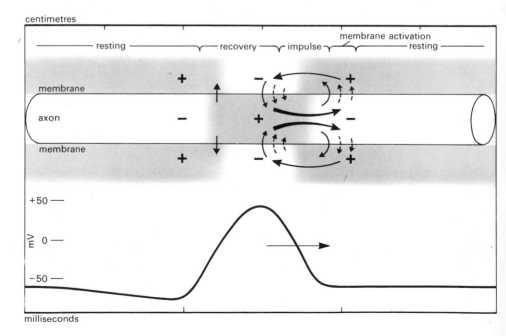

this in turn depends upon the size of the fibre (so that in larger fibres impulses travel faster), and upon whether the axon is covered with myelin, which speeds conduction even more dramatically.

## Junctions between neurones

Although by the turn of this century much was known or suspected about the transmission of impulses along nerve fibres, it was not known that nerve cells were separate entities. The prevailing view had been that the brain was a continuous network of nervous fibres, allowing the passage of impulses throughout the nervous system. The neurone theory, that nerve cells were separated from each other, was established by the microscopist Santiago Ramon y Cajal. Working with a technique for staining nerve tissue invented by Camillo Golgi, Cajal finally succeeded in convincing his contemporaries that both axons and dendrites had free endings.

In Golgi's technique the whole extent of perhaps

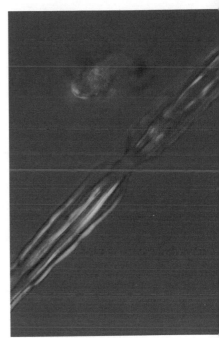

*Above: speeds of conduction in nerve fibres vary. In man the fastest fibres conduct at speeds round 300 feet per second, while the slowest conduct at about 2 feet per second. In the high-speed fibres the nerve impulse jumps between the gaps in the myelin sheath (seen in this picture), where the membrane is uninsulated. Slower-conducting fibres have no myelin*

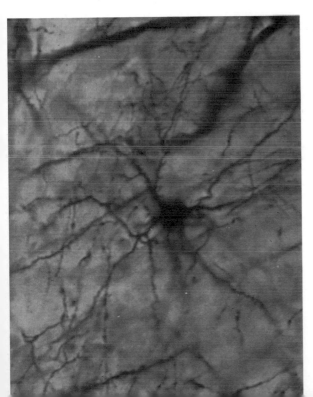

*A modern photomicrograph made from one of Cajal's original Golgi-stained slides showing a typical cortical cell*

one in every hundred neurones in a slice of brain (it is still not known why any particular cell is affected) becomes impregnated with silver, and is thus easily seen under the microscope. Golgi interpreted his own work as supporting the theory that all nervous fibres were continuously joined and in 1906, when both he and Cajal received the Nobel Prize, both took the opportunity to give speeches which attacked (albeit in polite tones) the other's theory. Since Golgi's and Cajal's work the electron microscope has revealed the membranes which Cajal thought did, and Golgi thought did not separate nerve cells, together with a great deal of other detail about the structure of synapses.

Calculations based on the electrical properties of nerve membranes show that at the vast majority of synapses nerve impulses could not possibly jump across the gap between cells. Therefore another means for transmitting the neural message at these places must exist. What happens is that when the nerve impulse reaches the end of an axon it triggers the release of a small quantity of chemical transmitter substance. The chemical diffuses across the tiny gap between the two neurones (about one fiftieth of a micron) and produces an electrical change on the membrane of the other neurone.

The existence of chemical transmission began to be suspected at the beginning of this century, when the neurone theory was firmly established. A chemical mediator released from nerves which acts on the muscle of the heart was unequivocally demonstrated by Otto Loewi at the University of Graz. Loewi said that his insight about chemical transmitter substances came to him while asleep (such is the sleeping as well as the waking life of scientists). He apparently awoke one night with the fully formed idea that the slowing down of the heart that occurs when one of the nerves supplying it (the vagus) is stimulated, was due to a chemical substance, and that if he bathed the heart of a frog during this vagal stimulation, some of the substance would diffuse into the fluid, which he could then apply to the heart of another frog. Feeling the idea was important he scribbled it down on a piece of paper, and went to sleep again. But next morning he could not decipher what he had written, and went about all day in a distracted manner. The next night he again awoke, fortunately with the same idea. However this time he did not allow it to evaporate and was later able to go to his laboratory and demonstrate the transfer of the chemical heart-slowing substance from the vagus of one frog to the heart of another. He also detected, in a similar experiment, a different substance released by the cardiac accelerator nerves which act to speed up the heart.

It was not long before it was found that chemical messengers not only provided the communication between nerve and muscle (in the heart and elsewhere) but also the communication between nerve and nerve. From Loewi's experiments, reported in 1921, a whole new area of research emphasizing the importance of biochemical events in the brain was opened up.

What is thought to happen when a nerve impulse reaches the synapse of an axon is that, by a mechanism that is not completely understood, a number of tiny containers (vesicles) release the transmitter substance that they contain into the synaptic gap. These vesicles can be seen in electron micrographs. A nerve impulse arriving at an axon terminal releases transmitter from

*Synaptic vesicles can be seen in the axon terminals, and synapses are often marked by slight thickenings of the membrane. The diagram shows the main features of the same synapse as is shown in the electron micrograph*

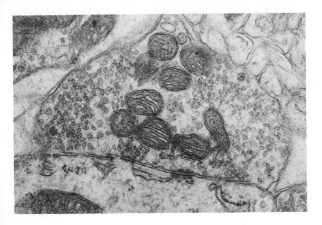

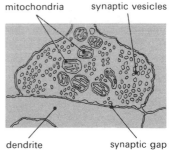

mitochondria     synaptic vesicles

dendrite     synaptic gap

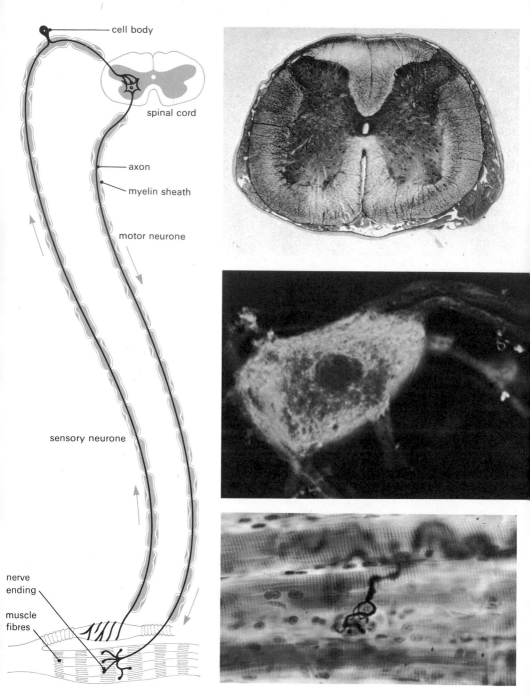

cell body

spinal cord

axon

myelin sheath

motor neurone

sensory neurone

nerve
ending

muscle
fibres

several dozen vesicles, and the effect of this transmitter on the next, so-called post-synaptic, cell is to alter the permeability of its membrane, and hence produce a flow of ions and an electrical change.

By the early 1950's it had become possible to record from inside much smaller cells than the giant neurones of the squid. Micropipettes, made by pulling out fine glass tubing under controlled heat, can be produced so that the diameter of the end of the pipette is only about half a micron. Filled with a conducting solution, these micropipettes can be used as electrodes and gently pushed inside cell bodies without apparently doing any damage. Of course both the tip of the micro-electrode and the cell into which it is inserted are too small to see, and in an experiment the micro-electrode is simply lowered into the required part of the brain. At the moment when the tip enters a neurone the characteristic 60–70 millivolt negative resting voltage is recorded: the sign that the tip of the electrode has penetrated inside a neurone.

The major experiments investigating the electrical effects of chemical transmission were performed by J. C. Eccles and his colleagues in Australia and New Zealand. They involved placing electrodes inside the large neurones whose axons directly supply muscles. The dendrites and cell bodies of these large motor-neurones in the spinal cord are covered with synapses from axons running down from the brain, from axons of intermediate neurones in the spinal cord, and importantly for these experiments, directly from nerve fibres supplied by sense organs in muscles. The whole arrangement of sense-organ connected via a nerve fibre and synapse to a motor neurone which runs to a muscle is a reflex pathway (discussed towards the end of this chapter).

In one experiment, Eccles applied stimuli to a nerve bundle in a way that allowed him to control how many axons in the bundle were activated with each stimulus. Each axon ended on a motor neurone, and released transmitter substance at its synapse when an impulse arrived. When Eccles stimulated only a few axons,

*Opposite: diagram illustrating a reflex pathway such as that studied by Eccles. When sensory fibres from stretch receptors are stimulated post-synaptic potentials are produced, and the impulses initiated in the motor neurones normally bring about a response appropriate to the sensory event that has occurred. Top: a cross-section of the cat's spinal cord. The dark H-shaped area contains many cell bodies of neurones while surrounding it are the tracts of fibres running up and down the cord. Centre: a typical motor neurone from the spinal cord. From this kind of cell Eccles made his recordings of excitatory and inhibitory post-synaptic potentials. Bottom: a motor nerve ending on a muscle*

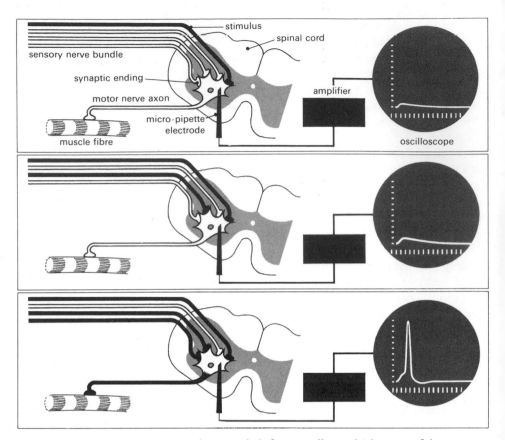

The effect of stimulating (black) more and more excitatory axon terminals is to increase the height of the post-synaptic potential. If the EPSP is large enough to reach threshold a new impulse will be fired down the motor axon

he recorded, from a cell on which some of the synapses occurred, a voltage that became slightly more positive just after the impulses had arrived, and he called this voltage change an excitatory post-synaptic potential (EPSP). When he stimulated more axons the EPSP got larger. When several synapses on any cell are stimulated at the same time the EPSPs spreading across the membrane of the dendrites and cell body combine and add together, so that the size of the total EPSP recorded within the cell depends on the number of active synapses. Not only is the EPSP different from the axon impulse in being of variable size, but it also lasts about fifteen times as long, thus extending the time over which events arriving from several synapses can add to each other.

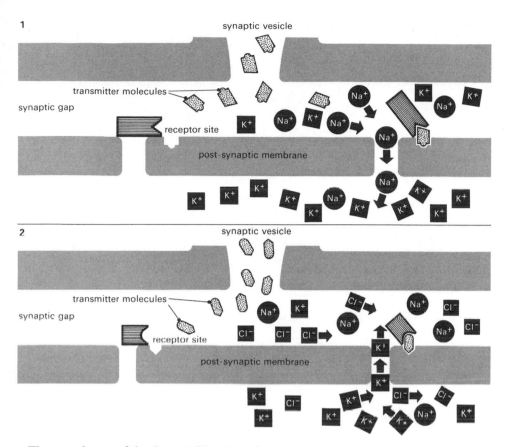

synaptic vesicle

transmitter molecules

synaptic gap

receptor site

post-synaptic membrane

2

synaptic vesicle

transmitter molecules

synaptic gap

receptor site

post-synaptic membrane

The membrane of dendrites is like that of axons in that it allows passive spread of electrical currents. If these passive currents travelling along dendrites and across the cell body reach the axon with sufficient size to achieve the threshold voltage then the axon will trigger, and a new impulse is produced. Since the first part of the axon has the lowest threshold of anywhere in the cell, this is where the impulse tends to begin.

In other ways dendrites and axons are rather different. The self-acting axon impulse works because making the voltage more positive increases membrane permeability allowing positively charged sodium ions to enter and change the voltage yet further positively, and so on. The permeability of the dendritic membrane at a synapse, however, does not depend upon the

*Transmitter molecules released into the synaptic gap open specific channels in the post-synaptic membrane. 1: excitatory transmitters allow sodium ions ($Na^+$) to pass, thus making the inside voltage more positive. 2: inhibitory transmitters make the membrane permeable to potassium and chloride ions ($K^+$ and $Cl^-$) thus short-circuiting the membrane*

voltage, but upon whether there is any transmitter substance on the membrane. EPSPs are produced by transmitters that increase the permeability of the membrane, allowing positive sodium ions in and decreasing the negativity of the inside voltage.

As Loewi demonstrated, there are also inhibitory transmitter substances, and Eccles has shown how these operate in neural synapses. Inhibitory post-synaptic potentials (IPSPs) are produced by transmitters which make the membrane more permeable to the positively charged potassium ions (which are mostly inside the cell) and also to the negatively charged chloride ions (which are abundant outside). The net result of the permeability changes is, as it were, to short circuit the membrane, by offering a very low resistance to those ions which tend to make the internal voltage more negative or to maintain it at the resting level. This prevents sodium ions from lifting the membrane voltage towards threshold. If EPSPs have already moved the voltage in a positive direction, IPSPs have a subtractive effect, and move the voltage back down towards the resting level. Thus when EPSPs and IPSPs spread towards the axon and combine they will respectively add to and subtract from the membrane voltage, and a new impulse will be triggered only if that voltage becomes sufficiently positive.

## The Cartesian reflex

A chain of communication through the nervous system has now been established. Impulses propagate unchangingly along axons and release transmitter substances at synapses. Transmitters produce excitatory or inhibitory potentials which add to and subtract from the resting voltage. If the combined post-synaptic potential changes to a sufficiently positive voltage, a new impulse is triggered. This is the pattern throughout the nervous system, from the receptors which produce electrical changes to trigger impulses in sensory nerves, through the synapses of the spinal cord and brain to the muscles.

In the same way that this understanding of nerve

*Opposite: different kinds of synapses can be distinguished by the shape and size of their vesicles. In this electron micrograph a synaptic ending (right) with round vesicles (presumed excitatory) and an ending (left) with rather larger and somewhat flattened vesicles (presumed inhibitory) make contact with the same dendrite*

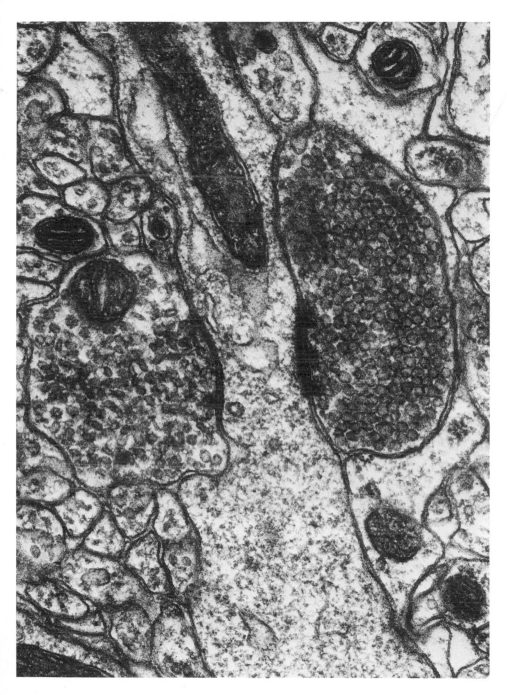

*René Descartes was not only father of modern philosophy but in some senses the father of modern brain research. He was the first to propose any kind of plausible mechanism of behaviour. Below: this statue, from a design of 1688, was arranged to squirt water at visitors. It was this kind of entertaining garden ornament that stimulated Descartes' explanation of reflex mechanisms*

transmission is dependent upon our knowledge of electrical and chemical processes, the very earliest account of the transmission of information from sense organs through the brain to the muscles was similarly influenced by the technology of the time. Descartes was the first to offer an account of neural mechanisms, and his explanation of how the brain worked was written in 1634, but published after his death. His ideas were much influenced by the water gardens that were fashionable in France at the time. A visitor walking in the gardens would step on particular tiles arranged to operate valves so that water flowed from a reservoir through pipes to operate various life-sized statues. If visitors 'approach a bathing Diana', Descartes wrote, 'they will cause her to hide in the rushes . . . or . . . they will cause a sea monster to appear and spew water in their faces, or similar things according to the whim of the engineers who made them.'

The nervous system, he supposed, was arranged on similar principles. Sense organs were operated by stimuli in the environment (just as were the tiles in the garden paths) and an external event acting upon a sense organ pulled tiny strings which ran within the nerves up to the brain. In the brain, the heart had pumped up a head of fluid which was stored in reservoirs (the ventricles). The strings opened valves to let this fluid run down the appropriate motor nerves (which were thought of as tubes) to inflate whatever muscles were appropriate for responding to the stimulus that had occurred.

Descartes in this way described quite succinctly the idea of the reflex, the means whereby because of careful arrangements of interconnections and switches (valves) an event in the environment causes the brain to make an appropriate response to it. For man, but not for animals, Descartes thought that a reasoning intellect (or soul), rather like the master engineer in the water garden, was stationed near the main reservoir in the brain, keeping an eye on things, and occasionally opening a few valves of its own.

As newer scientific understandings of the physical

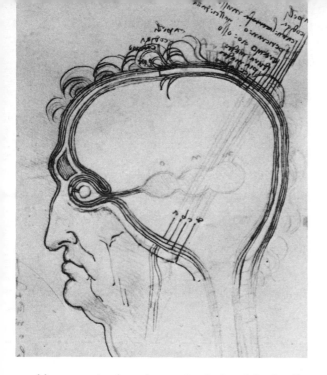

*Inside the brain are cavities containing fluid. This sketch by Leonardo da Vinci shows three ventricles, though he has not got their shape and position quite right. Descartes thought that the ventricles acted as a reservoir for fluid which ran through tubular nerves to inflate the muscles*

world were gained so the mechanical and hydraulic explanation of nervous processes was replaced by our present explanation in terms of electricity and chemistry. Though explanations of this kind now seem fairly complete, I have not in this chapter discussed anything that could not in principle be handled by a hydraulic system of valves and tubes. Fluid has simply been replaced by electricity, and the valves that determine the passage of this electricity have been identified as synapses.

We must recognize that the new electrical nervous system does not as such provide an explanation of the brain. It can provide only the first rung on the ladder of showing how information is collected by our sense organs and how re-routing operations of the brain can occur. More importantly, the idea of the brain as a re-routing device, either like an array of valves or like a more modern telephone switchboard, itself turns out to be inadequate, and much more powerful principles are needed to explain how we perceive, how we learn, or how we understand.

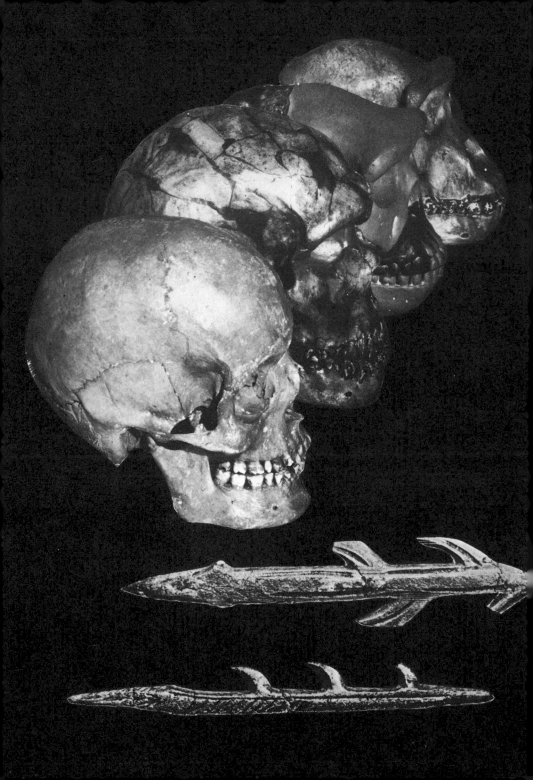

The *Guinness Book of Records* confers the record for the most brainless extinct animal on *Stegosaurus*, whose body weight was some $1\frac{3}{4}$ tons but whose plum-sized brain weighed only $2\frac{1}{2}$ ounces. Its brain weighed only four thousandths of one per cent of its body. In comparison, a typical estimate of the average brain weight of man is slightly over three pounds (1,360 g.), more than 2 per cent of the average body weight. Despite this, neither absolute brain size, nor size in comparison with the body is a good guide to intelligence, since the size, density of packing, and richness of interconnection of nerve cells varies considerably from species to species. In the nineteenth century there was nevertheless considerable interest in total brain size as an index of intelligence and in the relative sizes of parts of the brain as indicators of specific human faculties.

## The localization of function

It was Franz Gall (1758–1828) who seems first to have had the idea of paying attention to the size of various parts of the brain. Gall founded phrenology, and his speculations proceeded from a childhood observation that some of his acquaintances with particular gifts had heads of peculiar shapes. Gall taught that the brain was composed of several organs, each subserving a particular human ability (of which he supposed there were twenty-six or twenty-seven) and each situated in a particular part of the brain. Prominence of any faculty resulted in an enlargement of the correspond-

*Opposite: from right to left are skulls of a gorilla, Homo erectus, Neanderthal man, and Homo sapiens. There is a rough gradation of brain size from the gorilla to modern man, although some Neanderthals had a slightly larger brain capacity than Homo sapiens. More reliable evidence about the brain comes from examining 'behavioural fossils' such as tools or weapons of which these upper Palaeolithic harpoon heads are examples*

*Phrenology was not always taken seriously, as this nineteenth-century cartoon by 'L. Bump after J. Bump' shows*

ing area of the brain and hence of the part of the skull that covered it. Gall's ideas flourished for about a century. Though they were never wholly accepted in scientific circles, they had wide influence and did serve to establish, in Gall's phrase, 'the brain as the organ of mind'.

In the atmosphere created by phrenology it was natural for the skulls of great men to be studied after their death. One measurement made in this way was of Byron's skull which indicated his brain weight to have been about 2,000 g., much larger than average. It is easy to be impressed by this into thinking that brain size has something to do with genius, but plenty of other gifted men have had small brains and very ordinary men have had large ones. Although brain size has had a limited use in paleontology, we cannot by anatomical means be sure of telling the brain of a person with an IQ of 50 from that of a person with an IQ of 150.

The history of notions connecting the size of the whole or parts of the brain with various abilities is not without its funny side. After his death Gall's skull was subjected to careful scrutiny, and a phrenological biography notes that Gall's 'secretiveness was rather large but he never made bad use of it. He was too conscious of his intellectual powers to obtain his ends by cunning or fraud.' Though a man with considerable gifts, the unfortunate fact was that his brain was much smaller than average, and weighed only 1,100 g.

Although nothing of Gall's phrenological naming of parts of the brain now remains, he performed the valuable service to science of asking questions about the functions of parts of the brain.

*A typical phrenological map. After Gall's original enumeration of twenty-six or twenty-seven supposed organs, the number grew steadily until in this diagram there were forty-one. Of course, there is no reason why a list of such propensities should not continue growing indefinitely*

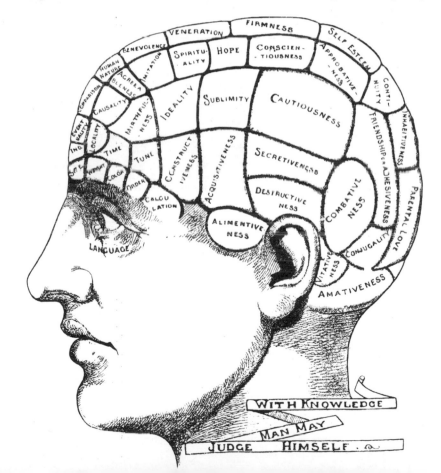

## Visible anatomy of the nervous system

Many of the parts of the brain which are visible to the naked eye from outside, or from ordinary dissection, had been given names long before there was any speculation about function. The ancient anatomists were therefore forced to choose an entirely arbitrary nomenclature. Of course, even mundane words sound exotic in a foreign language and since most of the names are in Latin this now disguises their ordinariness. Thus cerebral cortex simply means outside layer of the brain (cortex means outside covering), cerebellum means little brain, and so on. Perhaps it is fortunate that descriptive anatomy is so neutral with respect to function. Otherwise terminology might be continu-

*About 80 per cent of the human brain is occupied by the paired cerebral hemispheres, the surfaces of which are deeply convoluted, thus increasing the total area of cortex. Cut in half along the mid line, densely packed cell bodies (stained blue) surrounding tracts of axons (white) are revealed*

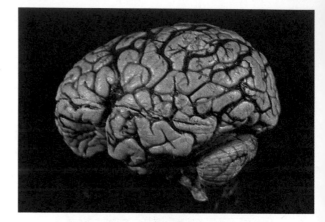

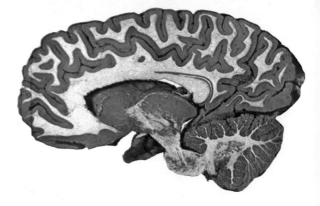

ally changing with the improvement of our ideas about how the brain works.

The human brain is a pinkish grey colour. It is furrowed on the outside and has a jelly-like consistency. The grey colour occurs where there are large aggregations of nerve cell bodies (the grey matter). Tracts of axons carrying information over long distances are white because of the axons' myelin covering.

Peripheral nerves, which are bundles of axons, transmit information to and from the brain or spinal cord, and brain and cord together form the central nervous system. One can recognize within the central nervous system extensions of peripheral nerves as routes of sensory or motor information. By following

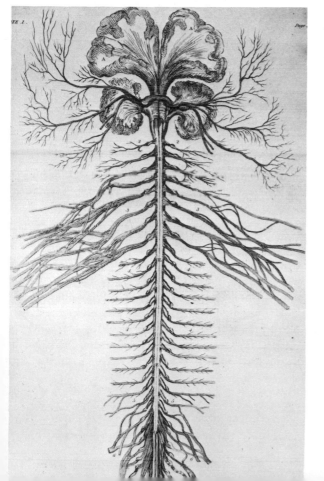

*Sir Charles Bell's diagram (1824) showing the peripheral nerves joining the spinal cord (E) and brain (A, B, C and D)*

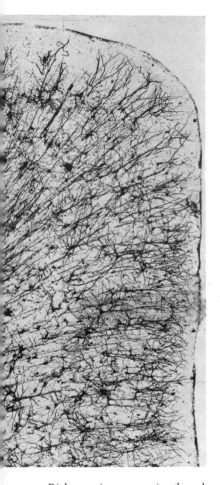

*Right: a microscope section through a small part of the cortex of the cerebellum (a small region at the rear of the brain concerned mainly with the control of movements) showing the characteristic deep folds. Under higher magnification (above) the neurones become visible. This section, made by D. A. Sholl and stained using a modification of the Golgi method, shows only about 1·5 per cent of the cells present*

these pathways one finds within the substance of the brain large groups (nuclei) of cell bodies with their many synapses. Finally, as we trace motor or sensory pathways through the brain we reach the cerebral cortex which also contains many cell bodies.

The cerebral cortex of man comprises the larger part of the outside surface of the brain. It is a deeply folded thin layer, between $1\frac{1}{2}$ and 3 mm. thick, i.e. up to the thickness of about forty pages of this book. If spread out flat it would have a surface area equivalent to between five and seven of these pages (most estimates of total cortical area in man are between 1,500 and 2,200 sq. cm). Within this space are some ten thousand million ($10^{10}$) neurones. The cortex in man is much more enlarged, in comparison with the rest of the brain, than in any other animal. It is in the cortex therefore that several generations of anatomists, starting with Gall, have very naturally localized the so-called higher functions. Later generations have often been more reticent than the phrenologists about where particular functions were located, but they have nevertheless often supposed the cortex to be the seat of our intellect and finer feelings.

## Electrical stimulation of the cortex

Since the time of Gall, anatomists have tried to find out about brain function in animals by observing the effects of electrical stimulation, and of the removal of various parts. One of the most striking pieces of research of this kind has been done on the human cortex by the neurosurgeon Wilder Penfield and his associates at the Montreal Neurological Institute.

Some operations upon the brain, for instance to remove cancers, do not necessarily require the patient to be completely anaesthetized. Instead a local anaesthetic can be used, cutting off sensation to the parts of the head that would be affected by the operation, but allowing the patient to remain conscious. Penfield and his colleagues took the opportunity offered by these operations to stimulate the surface of the cortex electrically with small voltages, and to ask the patient for his reactions to the stimuli. Since the surface of the brain has no sense organs, patients did not feel sensations actually in their brains during such manoeuvres. Instead, they referred to events with which the stimulated nerve cells were concerned.

Seemingly, Penfield was able to replace the fanciful functions suggested by Gall with functions suggested by these extremely direct demonstrations. When a strip of cortex running over the top of the cortex roughly between the ears was stimulated, the patient reported tingling sensations in various parts of his body, the location of the sensation moving from place

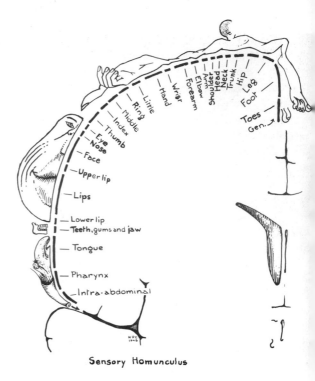

Sensory Homunculus

*A Penfield illustration showing a strip of cortex running across the brain from which sensations in various parts of the body are elicited. The extent of the areas for effective stimulation are indicated by the size of the drawing of each body part*

to place as the surgeon moved the tip of the stimulating electrode across the surface of the cortex. In this way it was possible to map out the area of the brain from which bodily sensations were elicited, labelling each spot with the part of the body in which the sensation was felt.

Not all points on the surface of the brain gave rise to skin sensations. Stimulation of an area at the back of the brain produced the sensation of lights, flashes streaks, colours and visual movements. On another part of the cortex, at the side of the head, stimulation induced the patient to hear sounds.

Although all of the sensations produced were compelling and vivid, none of them was ever described as arising from a real object or event in the outside world. When a patient reported a sensation on the thumb, he never believed that something actually touched his thumb. The lights and flashes were never described as seen objects.

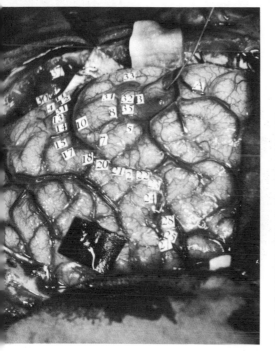

A strip of cortex just in front of the area from which skin sensations had been elicited was found to be capable of producing movements (confirming many previous experiments on animals). Stimulation at one point might make the patient's finger move, at another his lower leg. At yet another a vocal movement producing a sound would occur. These fragmentary movements were involuntary. The patient could feel himself making them, but could do nothing to stop them. In yet other areas of the brain, stimulation stopped speech in mid-sentence, induced feelings of unreality or even produced vivid hallucinations. Across large areas no effects were found at all – the 'silent areas' of the brain.

Like Gall before him, Penfield produced a map of the brain. Though his demonstrations are more convincing and certainly more dramatic than Gall's correlations of cranial protuberances with the idiosyncrasies of his acquaintances, we must beware of falling into the

*Left: the numbered tickets represent points from which positive responses (mostly movements and sensations) to electrical stimulation were obtained in one of Penfield's operations (This patient was found to have a tumour between A and B.) Above: Penfield's map of the localization of cortical function. Though some of it is based on firmer evidence than Gall's it may still be quite misleading*

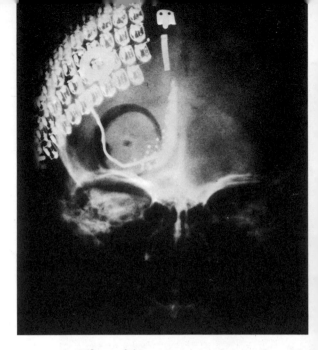

*An X-ray of the skull of a blind woman showing electrodes, each equipped with a tiny radio receiver, which had been permanently implanted by Brindley and Lewin to see whether the eyes could be circumvented by electrically stimulating part of the cortex. Though small points of light were 'seen' on stimulation, the technique does not look too promising for reinstating perception*

same trap. Effects of damage or stimulation of specific parts of the brain indicate that these parts are involved in certain sensory, motor or other activities, but not that they are solely responsible for them. The idea that if stimulation or removal of some area results in disturbances of speech, that area is therefore the speech centre is quite misleading. Although various groups of interconnected nerve cells no doubt have particular functions, it is not known what such elementary functions might be. Nor is it known that cells with a common function are all in one area, nor indeed that, if involved in one function, they are not also involved in others. Although most people have found it not too difficult to reject the notion that various parts of the brain are responsible for such functions as 'acquisitiveness' (which Gall described as well developed in pickpockets) many have accepted equally implausible suggestions that particular areas are the centres of speech, sleep and so on.

The mistake arises from supposing that if the brain is the organ that generates behaviour, then if we can separate behaviour into discrete categories, the brain too must be divisible into parts each separately responsible for one category of behaviour. We can easily see that this is a mistake by thinking about any moderately complicated mechanism with which we are familiar, for instance a motor car. Its behaviour can easily be categorized in various ways, e.g. speediness, hill-climbing ability, noisiness and so forth, or if one prefers less phrenological categories: going forward, going backwards, back-firing, etc. However, none of the functional components of the car is alone responsible for any of the whole car's behavioural attributes. This does not mean that parts of the car have functions which are unconnected with its behaviour. It is simply that the functions of the parts are described in quite different terms, and at what may conveniently be called a lower level. For instance, the distributor applies a voltage to the spark plug of each cylinder in turn so that the mixture of fuel and air is ignited at the correct point in each piston stroke. It is the combined operation of such lower-level functions that makes the whole engine work. We understand the car in terms of how electrical and mechanical components with defined properties interact to produce in various circumstances the whole gamut of motor vehicular behaviour.

No conceivable arrangement of attributes such as 'speediness' or 'going forwardness' could give a satisfying account of how a car works, and no similar set of behavioural descriptions will allow us to understand the brain. What we would like to know is how nerve cells (or networks), with defined properties at a lower level, are connected so that sequences of behaviour are produced by virtue of these properties and connections.

This is not to say that Gall's questions and Penfield's answers have not been valuable. Stimulation and lesions of the brain indicate firstly that it is meaningful to assign behaviour to certain categories in that, by using these techniques, particular aspects of behaviour can be selectively elicited or destroyed. Secondly, these methods indicate something of the routes that information takes into and through the brain.

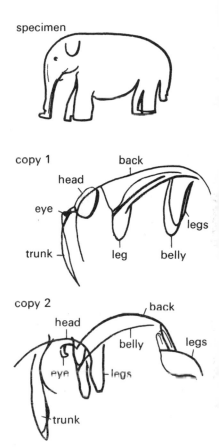

*An interesting and possibly important effect of damage and stimulation of the brain is that it sometimes breaks behaviour down into surprising components. These drawings by a patient who had received a wound in the cortex at the rear of the brain show that in trying to copy the elephant he could draw individual parts quite well, but could not put them together to make a whole*

Information enters the brain at receptors, each of which is responsive to one particular type of information such as light, sound, pressure, and so forth. At each receptor, one aspect of the information arriving, usually the intensity or the rate of change of intensity, is translated into a neural code that can be handled by the nervous system, and this process is known as transduction. It is familiar in many artificial instruments. A thermometer, for instance, transduces temperature into the length of a column of mercury, a code that can easily be compared by eye against a scale. A microphone is a more sophisticated transducer and produces electrical changes that mirror the shape of the sound waves applied to it. Biological receptors similarly need to code environmental information into electrical changes, since electrical signals are the means of communication within the nervous system.

The process takes place in two stages. First there is an electrical change, somewhat the same as the postsynaptic potential at a synapse, the voltage of which reflects an aspect (e.g. the intensity) of the stimulus applied to the particular receptor.

In the ear the combined effect of these so-called receptor potentials from several thousand receptor cells responding to the pattern of sound waves can easily be recorded from a large electrode placed in their vicinity. The similarity of the neural transduction process to artificial ones is very close indeed, as was demonstrated in 1930 by E. Wever and C. Bray. They

*The microphone is a familiar arti-ficial transducer translating patterns of sound into electrical changes. A similar translation process goes on in every sensory receptor*

placed a recording electrode in a cat's ear, connected the electrode via an ordinary amplifier to their laboratory telephone system, and while one of them talked into the cat's ear, the other in a different room, listened to what he was saying through the telephone receiver. Though this demonstration relies upon the combination of many individual receptor potentials, the transduction process in each one is essentially the same. Furthermore, transduction into an electrical voltage occurs in every type of receptor.

## Sensory codes

At the next stage this receptor potential is translated into nerve-impulse code, for transmission to the next cell. The receptor potential triggers a succession of nerve impulses along its single axon. Since nerve impulses are all-or-nothing, clearly information cannot be reflected by their size. It can only be carried in the intervals between them. This neural code in the axon is therefore analogous to the method by which FM (Frequency Modulated) radio broadcasts are carried by variations of the intervals (or more correctly the frequency) of a carrier radio wave. In the nervous system a succession of nerve impulses may be thought of as the carrier, and a change of signal at the receptor is transmitted as a change in frequency of impulses travelling along the axon.

E. D. Adrian discovered this coding of stimulus intensity into impulse frequency in the 1920's at Cambridge. Working at first with apparatus that now seems rather primitive and cumbersome, he recorded from several kinds of sensory nerve fibre in different animals, while applying appropriate stimuli to the receptors. He stretched the receptors in the muscles of frogs, applied pressure to receptors in the paws of cats and displayed lights (and even himself) in front of the eyes of conger eels. What he recorded in each case was trains of impulses.

He established that the codes in single axons from receptors, and those sent to muscles were exactly the same. He also found two major varieties of receptor. One type responded to a stimulus by firing repetitively and steadily, reflecting the continued presence of the stimulus by a continuous sequence of impulses. In other types of receptor when the stimulus appeared (or

*Adrian's apparatus consisted of an amplifier which applied a voltage to a small column of mercury in a capillary tube dipping into sulphuric acid. The voltage changed surface forces acting on the mercury which therefore moved, and its shadow was recorded on a photographic plate which was pulled in front of the projector, thus tracing a graph of voltage against time*

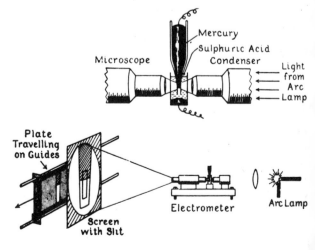

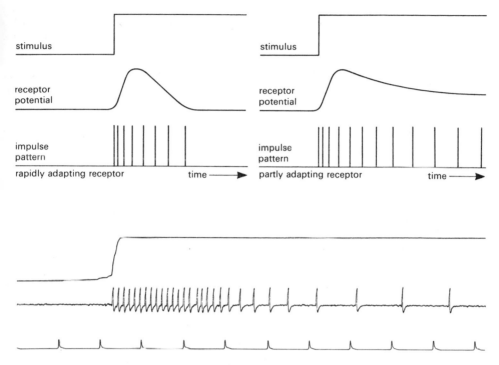

disappeared) it was reported by a burst of impulses which died away. In these fibres the signal was said to undergo adaptation. In fact, even continuously responding receptors adapt partially in that the maintained presence of a stimulus is reported by a lower rate of firing than its arrival.

Though one cannot directly observe sensory signals in oneself this adaptation process can be experienced by placing the hand, palm downwards, on a table to keep it steady, and then laying (or getting someone else to lay) a light object such as a pencil on the back of the hand. You can feel the pencil arrive, but its continued presence very quickly becomes undetectable. A heavier object, or something hot or cold excites different types of receptor which adapt incompletely or more slowly, so that such objects can be detected for longer. If a movement of the hand is made, this, of course, changes the stimulation of the receptors and new impulses are fired. Rather than representing a

*Top: adapting and partially adapting receptor action; the height of the receptor potential is translated into impulse frequency in each case. Above: response of an adapting pressure receptor (middle trace) to an applied pressure (top trace). The time marks (lower trace) are 25 msec apart*

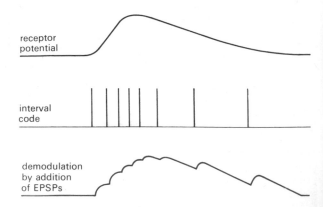

receptor
potential

interval
code

demodulation
by addition
of EPSPs

*At a synapse, if each impulse produces a small EPSP, the EPSPs summate and demodulate the impulse code, producing a potential of similar shape to the graded potential that generated the impulses in the previous neurone*

regrettable loss of information, adaptation seems to indicate an important principle. Many receptors respond primarily to change, and sensory channels are thus reserved for new events; things which have been there for some time cease to be of importance.

Since Adrian's research it has been found that adaptation in receptors (either complete or partial) occurs as a dying away of the height of the receptor potential. At the receptor, impulses are triggered along the axon at a rate proportional to the height of the receptor potential. At the end of the axon, at an excitatory synapse, these impulses produce EPSPs, which add together to make a potential with a shape very like that of the receptor potential. The synapse thus demodulates the impulse-frequency code just as a radio set demodulates an FM radio signal.

If nothing else were happening at that particular nerve cell the combined EPSP would act just like a receptor potential and trigger a series of new impulses along the axon, so that the same information was carried in the pulse-frequency code along the next axon.

However, nerve cells do not merely decode the impulse signal, and then recode it again. While the signal is contained in the post-synaptic potential the information can also be processed, added to or subtracted from, by other excitatory or inhibitory signals arriving at other synapses. The nerve cell can perform logic, and will for instance send out new pulses along its axon

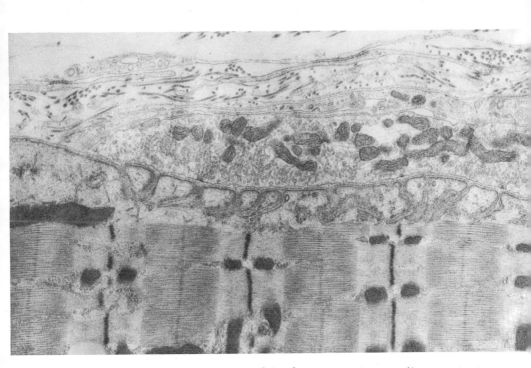

only if at its many input terminals excitation sufficiently outweighs inhibition.

If a suitable pattern of impulses reaches a particular set of synapses, then the neurones concerned will direct an appropriate pattern of nerve impulses to the muscles. Muscles also read the pulse-frequency code, in much the same way as does a synapse. Each fibre of a multifibre muscle contracts with a strength proportional to the rate of nerve impulses that it receives. In normal muscular movements, however, gradation of effort in a muscle is achieved primarily by controlling the number of active fibres, each of which is fed with impulses at a relatively standard rate.

How the electrical signal in a muscle is transformed into a mechanical contraction need not concern us here. More important for brain research is the question of what constitutes a meaningful pattern of nerve impulses, and how a set of nerve cells recognizes it and activates the right muscles to produce appropriate behaviour.

*A single nerve fibre transmits its excitation via synapses usually to several muscle fibres. In this micrograph a long axon terminal containing mitochondria and vesicles can be seen in contact with the membrane surrounding a single muscle fibre. The impulse code is demodulated by the muscle and (below) traces of four patterns of contraction with progressively higher frequencies of impulses are shown superimposed*

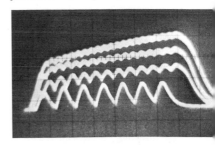

## Reflexes

Charles Sherrington, the British physiologist who worked at the end of the last century and the beginning of this, was the first to give any answers to these problems that were conceptually more advanced than those given by Descartes 250 years before him. Nevertheless, despite Sherrington's work Descartes' account of brain mechanisms (except for the change in technological language from hydraulics and mechanics to electronics) is not very different from the one still held by some neurophysiologists and psychologists today.

Most of Sherrington's experiments were on decerebrate animals, which had had their brain severed from the spinal cord by an operation. This left the limbs and senses of the main part of the body intact, though no longer communicating with the brain.

Descartes had thought that animals were without a reasoning soul, that they were puppets that responded automatically to the environmental stimuli that pulled

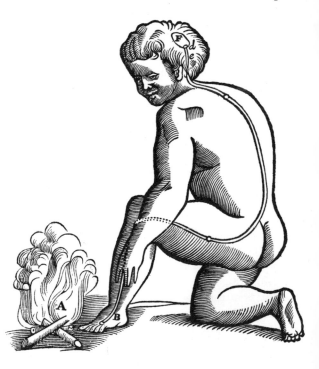

*An illustration from Descartes' book Traité de l'Homme showing how reflex withdrawal of a limb from a fire might be achieved. The fire causes a thread to be pulled in the nerve (B) opening a pore (d) in the brain. Fluid flows from the ventricle reservoir (F) to the muscles in the foot, causing it to be withdrawn*

the strings attached to their sense organs. Man was different in that his reasoning soul or mind (Descartes' world *l'âme* means either or perhaps both) could also influence the opening and closing of valves to let fluid into the muscles. Sherrington has remarked, rather in the manner expected of a member of a pet-keeping nation, that 'Descartes can never have kept an animal pet.' However, he continued, the decerebration operation puts 'within reach of the observer a puppet-animal that conforms largely with Descartes' assumptions'.

What was so interesting about Sherrington's experiments was that even with these simplified puppet-animals, the activation of a reflex depended not on some very simple stimulus that 'pulled a string' in some nerve fibre or set of nerve fibres, but on very complex patterns of information. Furthermore, reflex responses were well defined and purposeful movements.

One of the reflexes studied by Sherrington (previously used by Descartes to illustrate his view of neural mechanism), was the withdrawal of a limb from a painful stimulus. All that seemed to be required was that special receptors sensitive to pain sent impulses to cells in the spinal cord, which directed (or, to use the earlier term, reflected) the impulses towards those muscles which made the withdrawal movement.

Simple and obvious as this explanation may seem, it just will not do. Though one set of muscular contractions will be used for withdrawing a paw or a hand from one position, different muscles, or muscles acting in a different combination, have to contract in a different way in order to withdraw the hand when it is in another position. Even for the simplest reflexes the nervous system 'thinks' not in terms of contracting specific muscles, but of making specific purposive movements. The pattern of nerve impulses sent to the muscles, contracting the right muscle fibres, with the right time intervals between each part of the movement is both complicated and appropriate to the circumstances.

As it happens the neural signal that indicates pain,

A splendid picture of Adrian (left), Forbes, another pioneer of modern electrophysiology (right), and Sherrington (centre) taken in 1938. Sherrington's comment on being shown this photo by Forbes was, 'You and Adrian are having an argument and I – looking like the gargoyle I am – am wondering who is right.'

and which initiates the withdrawal reflex, is not just nerve impulses in some special nerve fibres. It too is a pattern. In fact, all the information we have about the world from our receptors comes not via impulses as such, but arises as neural mechanisms recognize patterns as having particular meanings, and interpret particular arrangements of impulses in many fibres as arising from objects or events in the world.

Another of Sherrington's studies concerned a reflex in which the animal pushed out its leg when pressure was applied to the underside of its paw. Neither Sherrington, nor anyone since, has been able to stimulate either the skin, or the sensory nerve electrically with any kind of artificial pattern to elicit this reflex. Although the same nerves are surely stimulated electrically as are stimulated by pressure on the paw, the nerve cells in the spinal cord recognize only certain patterns of impulses as signifying pressure, and having recognized it, organize the appropriate thrusting movement.

In the same way Penfield's patients (discussed in the previous chapter), electrically stimulated in particular areas of the cortex, felt tingling sensations in their skin, but never thought that anything was actually touching them. Just as some collections of letters or words are meaningless, some patterns of impulses (such as are produced by electrical stimulation) are neural gibberish, and neither the brain nor the spinal cord can interpret them as coming from anything real; which of course is absolutely correct.

One gives oneself just such a meaningless sensation when one bangs an elbow, artificially stimulating a sensory nerve running from the little finger and part of the finger next to it, up the arm and over the bony protuberance of the elbow. It is not inappropriate that this should be called banging the funny-bone; 'funny' of course meaning 'odd' or 'strange'. One can give oneself another meaningless or strange sensation by closing an eyelid and pushing gently with a finger on the skin in the corner of the eye. A patch of light can then be seen on the side opposite the finger. What is happening is that the brain is fooled because pressure of the finger triggers off receptors in the eye (just as pressure triggers nerve impulses in the 'funny bone'). Of course, the brain interprets it as light of some sort, because nerve impulses are always the same however they are initiated, and because the brain decides what kind of stimulus has occurred largely on the basis of knowing which fibres are connected to each kind of receptor. Also it interprets the stimulus as coming from the direction towards which the particular light-receptors look at the world. If the finger is moved about a bit, the patch moves. The nerve impulse pattern set up by prodding finger cannot however be interpreted as an object in the outside world. Just as when it organizes muscular contractions the brain 'thinks' in terms of movements, when dealing with sensory information it 'thinks' in terms of real things in a real world.

*Seeing stars – a familiar comic strip theme. The effect arises when receptors in the eye are energetically stimulated by pressure rather than light*

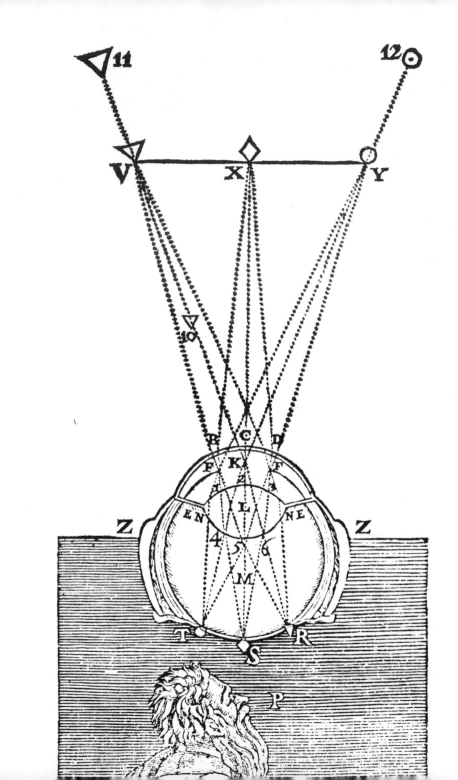

*

One of the most important things we have to understand about the brain is how networks of nerve cells detect patterns, and interpret them as arising from significant events or objects in the environment. If we take visual patterns as an example, an object such as a teacup can be recognized independently of colour, size, orientation, or position, and even of its exact type. One may perceive the same object on two different occasions, and yet the pattern arising from it of many impulses in many axons is probably never the same twice.

## Image formation

Before discussing how patterns are detected by neuronal networks I must describe how a pattern arising from the environment can be displayed on a spatial array of receptors so that it excites many nerve fibres to fire, each with its own temporal sequence of impulses. The sort of thing that occurs is most easily understood for the eye.

It is clear that some special apparatus is necessary in order to display different parts of the visual field on different receptors. The same problem arises in photography. Without the special apparatus of a camera, a photographic plate exposed in front of any visual scene would, when developed, turn out to be a uniform

*Opposite: Descartes was the first to investigate image formation by the eye. This illustration of 1637 shows how when the back of a bull's eye was removed and replaced with thin white paper an image of the scene at which the eye was pointing was displayed on it. A less messy way of doing the same thing is to put a piece of tracing paper in the place of the film of a camera, open the shutter and view the paper from behind*

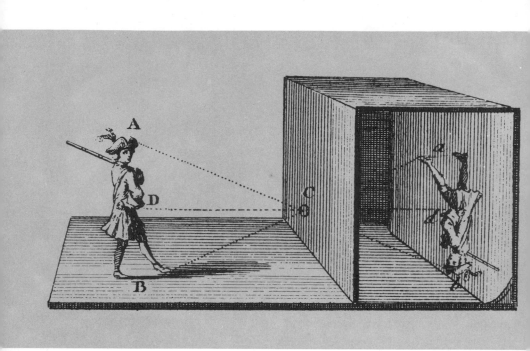

*This eighteenth-century engraving of a camera obscura illustrates image formation perhaps more clearly than Descartes' drawing. The modern camera is a development of the camera obscura, and both eye and camera form images in the same way*

grey. Formation of the image in the eye results in the visual field being projected in an orderly arrangement, but inverted, on the back of the eye upon the set of receptors and other cells that together make up the retina. Each of the 130 million receptors in each eye receives light from a particular point in the visual field. It does not, of course, matter that the image on the retina is upside down. There is no little man inside the brain who is going to have to inspect it. Instead there are networks of nerve cells which interpret a particular pattern from the receptors as arising from a teacup, or whatever, in the way that we normally experience it.

The receptors correspond in one sense to the photographic emulsion on the film in a camera in that they contain photo-sensitive pigment which changes when light strikes it. The extent of the change is signalled to the nerve cells to which the receptors are connected. At the same time the chemical changes of the pigment alter its colour. Unlike the photographic pigment

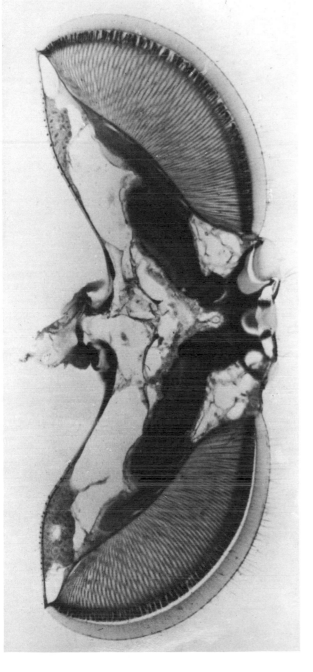

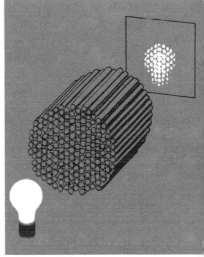

The compound eyes of insects form images quite differently from the eyes of vertebrates. Left: a section through a bee's two eyes, each made up of many tiny tubes equipped with their own photo-sensitive cells. The same principle is used in fibre optics, and can be modelled by blackening a large bundle of ordinary drinking straws with ink and holding the bundle up to a scene. This set of tubes will then transmit a very grainy image onto a piece of paper behind it (above)

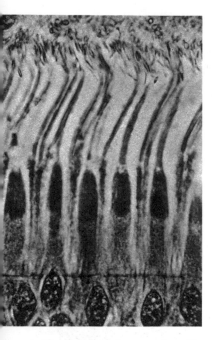

*Visual pigment is arranged on thin folded membranes (right) in the outer segments (narrow ribbon-like parts) of the receptor cells of the retina (above). This electron micrograph shows part of two adjacent receptors*

however, the receptor pigment can be reconstituted in a relatively short time, and re-used for detecting further changes in the light striking the receptor.

Just how like a photographic emulsion the pigment-containing receptors are has been shown by exposing the eye of an animal briefly to a visual scene and then fixing the image. Willy Kühne, professor of physiology at Heidelberg, took just such a snapshot in 1878. He arranged a rabbit so that it was looking out of a window. He then covered its eyes with a black cloth for a few minutes so that any pigment that had been changed by previous patterns of light falling on the eyes was regenerated. He then removed the cloth for three minutes, and immediately decapitated the rabbit, removed and cut open an eye and placed the retina in a solution of alum overnight. This fixed the visual image, and the next morning Kühne was able to come into his laboratory to see the photograph taken by the rabbit's eye upon the retinal receptors in which the pigment had been changed in colour by the light falling upon it.

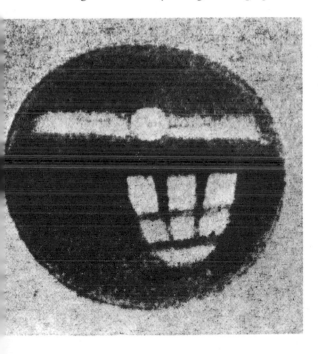

*Willy Kühne's drawing of a retinal photograph from a rabbit's eye. The pigment changes brought about by the eye looking at a window were fixed chemically, thus making the image visible on the retina. Kühne later performed a similar experiment on a guillotined criminal but was unable to identify the subject of the optogram*

This theme has been used in fiction: a murderer is identified by the image left in the eyes of the victim. The improbable part of this fantasy is that the murdered person should have had his eyes shut for some time, and then looked fixedly at his assailant who must have stood still for a minute or two before making his attack. The eyes of the victim would have had to be closed after recording their incriminating evidence and removed and fixed within minutes of death. When Browne and Kennedy murdered Police Constable Gutteridge in 1927, a macabre feature of the crime was that the victim's eyes were shot out – and it was said that the reason was this same superstition.

The retina of vertebrates contains not only the layer of receptors but four other layers of nerve cells, which all process information, so that by the time nerve impulses are sent up the optic nerve, visual patterns have already undergone extensive analysis. Thus the impulse traffic of the optic nerve does not merely transmit the image on the retina in neural terms.

The vertebrate retina develops as an outgrowth of the brain. In the embryo the brain starts as a hollow structure, with the pigment-containing receptors of the retina developing from cells on its inside surface.

*The eye develops from an outgrowth of the brain. Its final form is an image-forming sphere lined with a layer of receptors and other nerve cells*

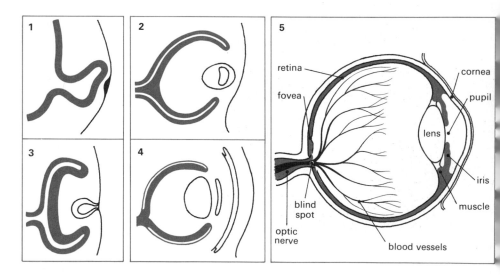

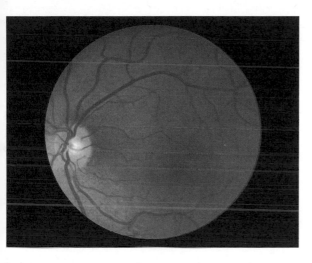

One result of this is that before light reaches the receptors it has to pass through four layers of nerve cells, as well as the network of arteries and veins that form the retinal blood supply. It is easily possible to see that the blood vessels of one's own eye lie in front of the receptors by shining a small torch through the skin at the corner of a lightly closed eye. A pencil torch or pocket torch is best for this because its bulb must be pressed gently onto the skin of the closed eyelid in the outside corner of the eye and then wiggled about a little. The shadows of the blood vessels will then be seen, extending like the branches of a tree.

Of course, shadows of the retinal vessels fall on the receptor layer all the time. When we look at them using a torch, light is cast from a different direction than usual, and a continuous movement of the light source is made so as to prevent adaptation. The reason why we are not usually aware of the vessels is partly due to adaptation, and partly due to the brain ignoring them. A similar thing happens for the blind spot. This is a part of the retina where the blood vessels and the fibres that make up the optic nerve tunnel through the receptive layer. There are no receptors at all on this patch, but we are nevertheless not normally aware of a gap in the visual field.

*Retinal blood vessels lie in the path of light to the receptors, and their shadows can be observed by shining a torch through the eyelid. They can also be seen by taking a photograph through the pupil. The pale disc from which the vessels radiate is also the point from which the optic nerve fibres leave (below) and it has no receptors (arrayed in the reddish bands to either side of the exit point). The result is that we are blind to images falling there*

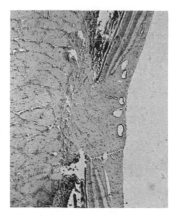

*If you close the left eye and look directly at the round spot with your right eye, holding the page about 12–15 inches from the eye, you will find that the cross, whose image then falls on the blind spot, disappears*

Demonstrations of the blind spot and the retinal blood vessels illustrate a rather profound principle of perception, namely that we make self-consistent interpretations of visual patterns as objects in the visual world. If we look at the world through a dirty window there is no temptation to categorize bits of dirt or reflections from the window as part of the scene outside. In an even more complete way there is no tendency to interpret the shadows of retinal blood vessels, or the obscuration of pieces of the external scene, as being part of that scene. Nor are we aware of the blind spot as a gap in it. Indeed obscured details of the outside scene seem to be constructed to fill the gaps, and parts of the image on our retina are rejected as incompatible with the whole scene. Though in the normal course we cannot see retinal blood vessels just by concentrating on them, we can concentrate on marks on the glass of a window, or on a reflection from it, but again each shift of attention is accompanied by interpretation of self-consistent parts of the image, and rejection of other parts as having no place in that scheme.

## Cells of the retina

The receptors of the retina connect to two other types of retinal cell. One type, the bipolar cell, conducts information directly towards the optic nerve, while the other, the horizontal cell, spreads laterally, perpendicular to the direction of the main flow of information. Anatomists in the past have been unhappy about the existence of laterally spreading cells in the retina, and about the fact that the vast majority of bipolar cells were connected to several or many receptors. These interconnections, they thought, could only result in coarsening the grain of the image, and would militate against the transmission of a high resolution picture to the cortex where, of course, were

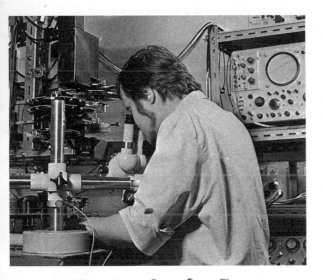

*Below: the retinal cells and their interconnections. The receptors (R) are of two types, rods and cones; horizontal cells (H) and amacrine cells (A) spread laterally across the retina while bipolars (B) and ganglion cells (G) conduct directly towards the brain. With amplifiers and oscilloscopes (left) electrical responses to light can be recorded from micro-electrodes inside the retinal cells of fish or amphibia, as shown below right. Only amacrine and the two types of ganglion cell show impulses – the other cells have graded potentials*

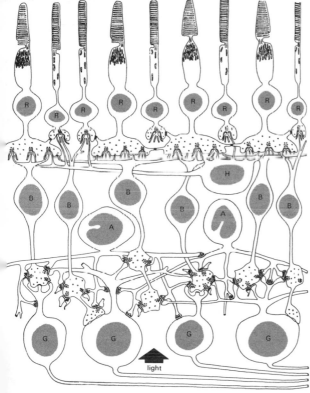

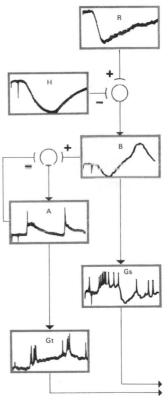

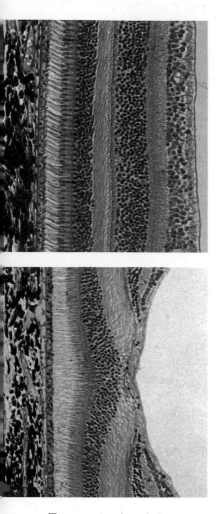

*Top: a section through the retina to show the layers of cells. The dark bands are the stained nuclei of (from right to left) ganglion cells, amacrine, bipolar and horizontal cells, and receptor cells. At the extreme left is the pigmented protective covering of the eye. Above: the central part of the retina, the fovea, where vision is most acute. Opposite: a single bipolar cell injected with dye*

lodged such inscrutable higher functions as perception. We now recognize that visual analysis does not take place only in the cortex but at every stage of the visual system. The lateral interconnections represent initial stages of this analysis.

Brain-ward transmission and lateral interaction occur again at the next stage in the retina. The bipolar cells synapse with retinal ganglion cells. There are about a million of these in each eye of man and their axons form the optic nerve. Spreading sideways, and making synaptic contact with many ganglion cells and many bipolars, are the amacrine cells.

The next part of this chapter will be devoted to discussing some of the functions that arise from the laterally spreading connections in the retina. Here we have very direct evidence not only for how the patterns of neuronal connection can give rise to detection of patterns of stimulation in the environment, but also of how nerve cells perform simple logical operations.

## Movement

Perhaps the pattern that is most important for all animals with brains is movement. Animals live in a world of threats and promise: something moving might represent either, and therefore demands action, even if only a second look. It is not surprising that the visual systems of animals from insects to man should be especially tuned to the pattern of movement.

If you get somebody to wave an object around far to the side of your field of vision (opposite the ear), then if you gaze straight ahead you will be able to see movement at the 'corner of your eye' even though you will not be able to identify the object. It is important not to take a covert glance at the object, and it is better not to hold it yourself; it is surprising how we build up a vivid visual impression of our environment not only by seeing, but by using other senses, and by knowing what must be there.

Evidently the pattern of movement, at the corner of the eye, can be recognized by the brain independently of recognizing what is moving. Indeed detection of

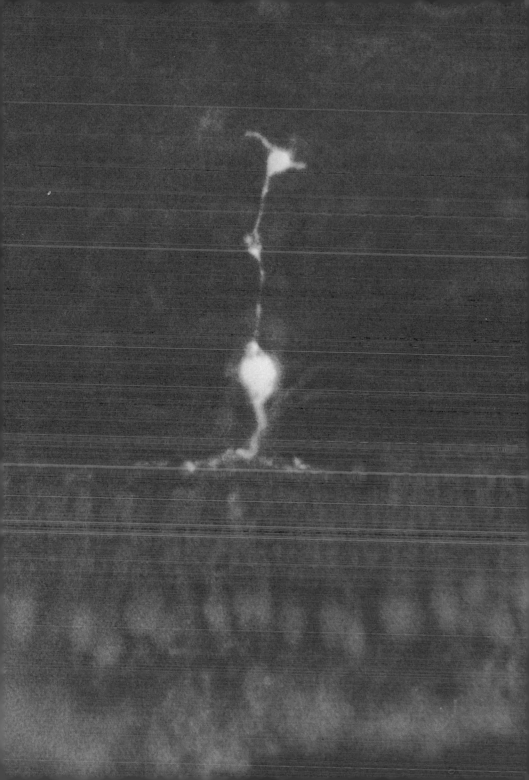

*A frog surrounded by insects will not catch and eat them unless they move, and it is likely that detection of movement constitutes a very large part of its vision*

*The familiar 'moving' neon signs of advertisements, fairs, night clubs, etc. are based on the brain's interpretation of a series of lights flashing in sequence as a single moving object*

movement is almost the only capacity we have in the most peripheral parts of our visual field. The same organization that we have in the periphery may represent the dominant arrangement serving the whole visual field of some more primitive animals. A frog, for instance, is said to starve surrounded by food so long as the food does not move, yet he will eagerly snap up a fly or a piece of meat joggled on a piece of string in front of him.

In the rabbit, an important part of the movement detecting apparatus lies within the retina itself. H. B. Barlow and W. R. Levick have made recordings from individual ganglion cells, and found that many of them fired a burst of impulses when a spot of light was moved across the retina in one direction, but remained unresponsive to stimuli moving in the opposite direction. The identity or shape of the moving stimulus did not matter much; these cells responded as well to a dark patch moving over lighter background as to a light patch moving over a darker background. Neither did it matter which particular set of receptors the moving light stimulated so long as it was within a certain part of the visual field, about half the size of a page of this book at arm's length, the area served by the cell from which the recording was made.

These cells responded to movement in a particular direction, independently of what was moving, making in effect a rather abstract judgement about the pattern of stimulation. What is more, these single cells could be misled in exactly the same way as an entire person is deceived by a spot of light flashed in one place and then almost immediately in another place nearby. Movement-detecting cells fire in response to such patterns and similarly we interpret events of this kind not as two lights flashing successively in different places but as a single moving light. It is upon this fact that many neon signs and other lighted advertisements, as well as the cinema, depend for their success.

It is not difficult to see what kind of neuronal networks would have the properties of detecting movement, either real or apparent. One needs to have cells in the second layer of the retina (or farther brain-wards in the visual pathway) which respond when stimulation of one set of receptors is closely followed by stimulation of another set not very far away. Neural connections might be made from one set of receptors directly to a cell in the second layer, but from the other set by a pathway over which transmission was delayed.

A movement-detecting cell might then be either of two types. It might be arranged to fire only if excitatory post-synaptic potentials reached it from both delayed and undelayed pathways at the same time; a pattern that would arise if a spot of light passed first over receptors connected to it via the delaying path, and then across receptors connected via the direct path. An alternative scheme would connect the movement-detecting cell so that the direct path would excite the cell but the delayed path would inhibit it. A moving spot stimulating first the delayed and then the direct paths would not fire the movement-detecting cell, as excitation and inhibition would cancel, but a light spot moving in the opposite direction would fire it.

Although the first of these schemes seems more straightforward, rather surprisingly Barlow and Levick's experiments show that movement detection by the rabbit works in the second way, since the movement-detecting cells were found also to respond to the flash of a single stationary light. If such cells needed both the delayed and undelayed input to make them respond then a stationary flash would not have been enough to excite them. If they detect directional movement by firing unless a stimulus operates first the delayed, inhibitory pathway and then the excitatory pathway, so making opposite post-synaptic potentials arrive at the same time and cancel, then such cells would respond to a stationary spot as well as one moving in the preferred direction.

Presumably movement detection in man follows the same general principle, although the relevant inter-connections are not in the retina but in the cortex. Far out at the side of the visual field where we can see

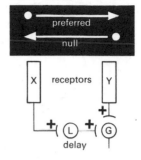

**1** logical operation X 'AND' L

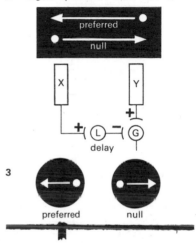

**2** logical operation Y 'AND NOT' L

**3**

preferred        null

*Two possible schemes whereby inter-connected neurones might detect movement by performing logical operations on input signals. 1: operation X 'AND' L (L is a laterally-spreading cell) causes a response to movement from left to right but not vice versa; 2: operation Y 'AND NOT' L causes response to movement in the opposite direction and is the scheme thought to operate in vertebrates' eyes. 3: impulses initiated by a spot moving in one direction*

*A spiral like this can be made by spinning a piece of paper on a gramophone turntable at 78rpm and moving a felt pen slowly sideways. The spinning spiral creates an impression of outward movement, but after inspecting this movement for thirty seconds or so when the spiral is stopped an illusory movement in the opposite direction will be seen, due presumably to adaptation of movement-detecting networks*

*Visible light is that part of the frequency band of electromagnetic radiation which has sufficient energy to cause chemical changes, but not enough to damage living cells. Though the spectrum looks coloured, light waves are not themselves coloured any more than the lower frequency radio waves or the higher frequency X-rays*

movement without knowing what is moving we can also detect a stationary flashing light. Such a flashing light does not look as if it is moving, but this may be because it stimulates many movement-detecting cells whose inhibitory pathways are laid out in all directions. Since no single directional set would be stimulated, no movement is seen. Evidently the perception of movement involves higher level operations in addition to those discovered in the retina of the rabbit.

Movement-detecting networks require the participation of interconnections spreading sideways. It seems perfectly plausible that in the rabbit either of the laterally spreading cell types, horizontal or amacrine, could mediate the delaying effect. Though the principle is firmly established, it is not certain at present which of these two types of cell is responsible.

## Colour

Although colour vision is an enormously complex subject, it is possible to sketch its outlines here in order to illustrate the theme of pattern detection by specifically interconnected retinal neurones.

Isaac Newton was the first to show that ordinary white light could be split into a rainbow of colours by passing it through a prism. The colours of the spectrum so produced correspond to different frequencies of electromagnetic vibration. Red lights correspond to the lower frequency (longer wavelength) end of the spectrum of visible light, while blue lights are of higher frequency (shorter wavelength). Glass prisms, and the raindrops that produce a rainbow, bend or refract light of higher frequencies more than light of lower frequencies, as it passes to the dense from the less dense substance.

Colour vision however depends not so much on the

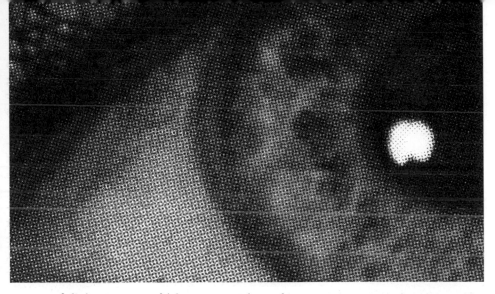

nature of light waves, which are not themselves coloured, but upon the nature of the receptors and interconnections of the retina and brain. We have three different types of light receptor capable of functioning in reasonably bright daylight. Each of these responds to light across the whole visible range of wavelengths, but each of the three types is most easily excited by one of three groups of wavelengths in the red, green or blue part of the spectrum.

It is as if each receptor were receiving light through a piece of either red, green or blue coloured glass. In fact the photosensitive chemical pigments in each receptor themselves act as the coloured filter, and absorb more light at some frequencies than at others. When any one receptor responds by producing electrical changes, it is not responding to colour as such, but merely to light intensity. However the effective intensity detected by any particular receptor type depends on the wavelength, because its pigment will absorb more of some wavelengths than of others. What we see as colour depends upon the proportions of the amount of light collected by the red, green and blue receptors. If a light falls on the retina exciting these receptors respectively in the ratio say 1:6:13 then this would be seen by the observer as a blue or blue-green colour.

*Colour printing depends on making mixtures of three basic colours, which (as explained by the Young–Helmholtz theory) can give the whole range of colour experience. Here a coloured print is enlarged to show that it is actually composed only of yellow, blue, red and black dots (black merely giving brightness)*

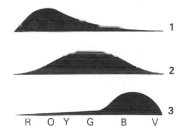

R  O  Y  G  B  V

*Helmholtz's development of Young's theory of colour vision is still the basis of our understanding of colour. His diagram shows how three types of cell (1, 2, and 3) each respond over the whole spectrum from red (R) to violet (V), but that each has a maximum in a particular place*

I say blue or blue-green, being rather deliberately vague, since colour exists in the mind of the beholder. It is his physiological and psychological processes which measure and operate upon this ratio of outputs from the three receptor types. Furthermore, since colour arises as an interpretation of these ratios, we have a system wide enough to encompass many more colours than occur as the visible wavelengths of light in a rainbow.

What we might look for in the brain is evidence of neural networks calculating these relative proportions. In the retina we do not find exactly that, but we do find evidence of what seem to be the initial stages of this colour analysis. Receptors have been found that do respond best to wavelengths corresponding to red, green and blue. Also neurones have been found that are excited by wavelengths in the red part of the spectrum, and inhibited by wavelengths in the green. Other cells are excited by yellow and inhibited by blue. Yet another class of cells is excited by all wavelengths, and thus responds to the total brightness of the light. The converse of each of these cell types has also been found; that is to say, there are cells excited by green and inhibited by red, and so forth.

These responses can be recorded from single horizontal cells in the retina, and the red-green and yellow-blue organization of so-called colour opponent processes is also found being transmitted through subsequent stages in the visual pathway.

Each colour opponent cell thus gives an output depending on the relative proportion or difference of its inputs, and one can imagine the sort of way in which the three types of receptor must be connected to produce these results. For instance, one type of red-green opponent cell would be inhibited by red receptors and excited by green. A blue-yellow opponent type is more complicated. Yellow requires the addition of inputs from both red and green receptors, which both make excitatory connections with the colour-opponent cell, while the connection from blue receptors is inhibitory. Cells responding to over-all bright-

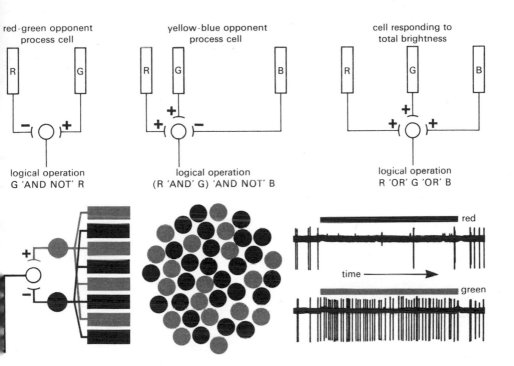

**red-green opponent process cell**

R  G

logical operation
G 'AND NOT' R

**yellow-blue opponent process cell**

R  G  B

logical operation
(R 'AND' G) 'AND NOT' B

**cell responding to total brightness**

R  G  B

logical operation
R 'OR' G 'OR' B

red

time ⟶

green

ness have excitatory (additive) inputs from all three receptor types.

The psychological reality of colour opponent effects, which was recognized nearly a century before their electro-physiological discovery, is displayed in the phenomena of complementary colours. A way of seeing one set of these is to stare at a patch of yellow, and then transfer the gaze to a grey area, which will then appear blue. Presumably, what occurs is that when looking at the yellow patch, red and green receptors are stimulated most, and this makes yellow-blue colour-opponent neurones fire (say) faster. As we continue to stare, the red and green receptors adapt, and when the gaze is transferred to a grey patch that stimulates the three receptor types more equally, the blue input will for a time predominate over the yellow, because the yellow (red + green) input is temporarily adapted, and hence diminished. The resulting predominance of blue input to yellow-blue opponent

*Top: three basic schemes give rise to two different types of colour-opponent cell and one brightness-detecting cell. Above: receptors sensitive to different wavelengths are intermixed in the retina, and in this recording from a ganglion cell of a ground squirrel, red inhibited the cell and green excited it*

cells makes them fire more slowly and this is interpreted as a blue colour. Similar phenomena occur with red-green opponent processes and similar explanations apply for cell types of the opposite kind to those just discussed, e.g. cells excited by blue and inhibited by yellow.

This organization of receptors and colour opponent processes does not constitute colour vision. It merely represents the most preliminary stages that are completed in the first two layers of cells in the retina. We know from a long history of psychological experiments that colour vision involves many other operations by the brain, of which something is understood in principle, although electro-physiological evidence is lacking.

*To see the colour complementary to yellow, stare at the spot at the centre of the yellow circle for about half a minute and then transfer your gaze to the centre of the grey square*

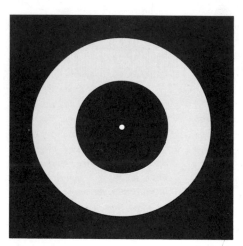
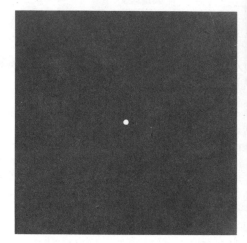

## Lines and edges

Perhaps the most famous experiments in the field of brain research during the last fifteen years have been those of David Hubel and Torsten Wiesel of Harvard University. Starting in 1959 they have worked through a theme which has excited everyone interested in understanding how neurones analyse information.

Their experiments were simple in conception. An

anaesthetized cat would be placed facing a screen upon which patches of light of various shapes and sizes could be projected. Through a small hole in the animal's skull a microelectrode would be lowered into the cortex until unmistakeable nerve impulses from a single cell were picked up by the recording system. Then, still recording from the same cell, light patches would be flashed and moved about the screen to define that cell's receptive field, the area of the whole visual field over which the activity of the cell could be influenced.

At this point came the unforeseen discovery. For most of the cells in the cortex the preferred stimulus within the receptive field was not the small round spot of light that had been used in almost all previous experiments on the physiology of the visual system. But for some cells it was a straight line; for others a straight edge. Though these cortical cells would respond to small light-spots to some extent, they seemed to be especially tuned to detect line segments, visual parts out of which seen objects may be composed. The skilful cartoonist can represent a complex scene with a few carefully chosen lines; the reason may be that these are exactly the kinds of element into which even more richly detailed images are broken down.

A particular cell in the area of the cortex to which the optic pathways directly connect would respond to a line (or an edge) only if it were tilted (oriented) in a particular direction, and only if it were projected on a particular part of the screen. Different parts of the visual field, and different orientations were served by other cells.

Some cells in this area, and many more in an adjacent region of the cortex, had yet more abstract properties. Hubel and Wiesel called them complex cells to distinguish them from the simple ones just described. A given complex cell responded either to a line or an edge in a particular orientation just like a simple cell. Unlike the simple cell though, it would not respond at all to small round spots of light. It would, however, respond to a line or edge in its preferred orientation

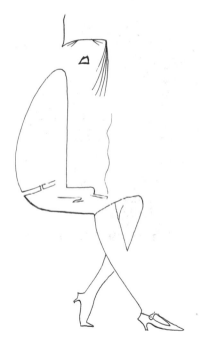

*A few simple lines can suggest a wealth of meaning. Can this fact have anything to do with the visual system's analysis of patterns into line segments?*

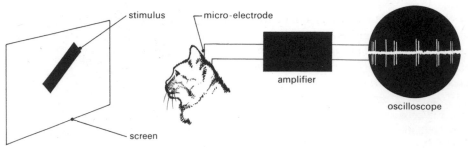

stimulus — micro-electrode — amplifier — oscilloscope — screen

*Above: the recording arrangement used by Hubel and Wiesel to investigate visually-responsive cells in the cortex of the cat. The impulses on the oscilloscope trace indicate firing of the cell. Right: this cell responded to a vertical edge in its receptive field (dotted line) but did not respond to other orientations. When the edge had its dark area to the right the cell was excited; with the dark area to the left the cell was inhibited but fired when the stimulus was turned off*

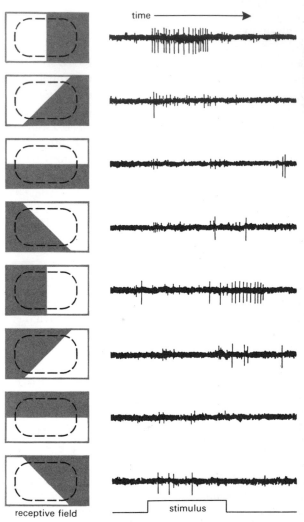

time ⟶

receptive field

stimulus

not just in one position but anywhere within the area of its rather large receptive field. The response of these cells was to stimuli slanted in a particular direction, somewhat independently of their precise position in the visual world.

This begins to satisfy one of the requirements for recognition of patterns, an invariant response to a pattern independently of position and of the particular receptors being stimulated. Hubel and Wiesel showed that some complex cells were also movement detectors, responding best to movement of the line or edge in only one of the directions perpendicular to the preferred line orientation. Movement detection in cats, monkeys and presumably man, takes place in the cortex, rather than in the retina, but the principle of subtracting a delayed from an undelayed set of inputs is probably the same as that described earlier.

Just as one can propose a diagram for connections of movement-detecting and colour-detecting cells, it is possible to see how Hubel and Wiesel's line-detecting cells might be connected to respond as they do. At the level of the ganglion cell the best stimulus for about half the cells is a round spot of light of some precise diameter and displayed upon a particular group of retinal receptors. Additional lights shone nearby diminish the response, and so does enlargement of the spot, because completely surrounding the excitatory area of the receptive field is an inhibitory area mediated by some of the laterally spreading cells of the retina. The other 50 per cent of the ganglion cells respond to a dark spot in their centre, and are inhibited by darkness on their surround. This so-called lateral inhibition mechanism adapts the retina to the locally prevailing level of illumination, and ensures that ganglion cells respond primarily to changes in illumination, such as are caused by spots, lines and edges, or by light being switched on or off. The best stimulus is therefore a light of a size that just fills the excitatory area while not invading the inhibitory region, changing suddenly in brightness or position. Already with this organization the ganglion cells are pattern-selective.

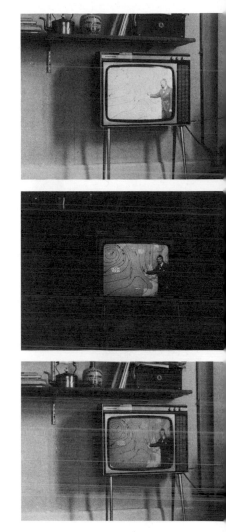

The eye responds to illumination changes about local average levels. A camera has to be set for overall illumination so here either the television screen is overexposed (top) or the room is underexposed (centre). We might see the scene as in the bottom picture which is in fact a photographic trick

A diagram to show the stimulus to which cells in the visual system seem especially tuned (the adequate stimulus), the shape of the receptive fields, a scheme of possible interconnections between cells and the types of logical operation performed by each type of cell

At the next set of cells in the visual pathway (in the lateral geniculate nucleus) the circular organization of centre and inhibitory surround is repeated. Just like the ganglion cells, about half these neurones have a centre excited by a dark patch on a lighter ground, and half have a centre excited by light on a darker background.

The next stage in the visual pathway is the visual cortex, in which the simple cells can be imagined as connecting to a row of the circularly organized cells at

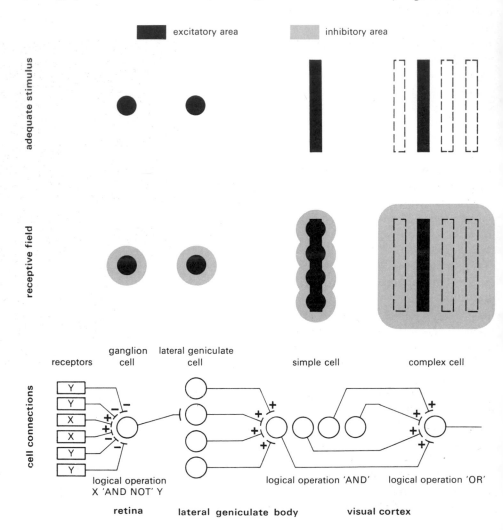

the previous level, firing best if all the cells in that row are stimulated. The even more abstractly selective complex cells may acquire their properties from being connected to a number of simple cells with the same preferred orientation, and covering an area of the visual field. The complex cell would then be operated by any one simple cell to which it was connected, in any position within its receptive field.

Hubel and Wiesel have gone on to discover further cells in areas of cortex adjacent to those that they first studied. These have further properties, for instance responding specifically to lines in a particular orientation, and independently of position, so long as the lines end or change direction at some particular point in the field. Cells with these even greater abstracting powers they have called 'hypercomplex' and (running short of terminology) even 'higher order hypercomplex'.

An important point about the cells which detect patterns by responding specifically to colour, movement, or line-segments, is that the cells owe their detection properties entirely to their synaptic connections.

## Pattern recognition

There are some who believe that the success of single neurone recording in continuing to discover cells with specific and abstract response properties solves all the problems of pattern recognition and perception. The principles whereby neurones are interconnected in such a way as to give them these properties are not complicated and several further examples are known.

To some it seems possible that as the microelectrodes prod into the cortex yet further and further from the area where the optic pathway enters, the response properties of successively higher orders of hypercomplex cells will be found to be more and more selective. Will there one day be found cells in the cat's cortex specifically responsive to a mouse, independent of its position, of its distance from the cat or whether it is a brown or a white mouse? Will there finally in the

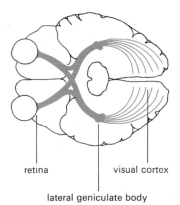

retina                    visual cortex

lateral geniculate body

*A schematic diagram of the visual system showing the anatomical location of each type of cell featured in the diagram opposite*

innermost recesses of the cat's brain be found a cell which can only be stimulated by the scene of a blazing log fire, in front of which is a thick-pile hearthrug and a bowl of milk?

The answer is no. In the first place, Hubel, Wiesel and others have inserted electrodes into other areas, and they find merely additional sets of line-detecting cells. However, if cells were responsive to a very specialized stimulus it would take almost infinite time and patience to find out what it was, trying first one thing, then another.

More important reasons why these principles of neuronal organization cannot simply be extended indefinitely to explain perception are provided by the psychological facts of perception. Some of these considerations were raised when discussing why we do not usually see our retinal blood vessels. To take just one further simple example: though we can understand how cells must be connected to detect movement of a spot or a line we do not understand how we ascribe movement to a spot projected onto a screen when the screen moves and the spot stays (physically) stationary. This illusion was invented by Karl Dunker, a psychologist of the Gestalt school. Gestalt psychology, which flourished in the 1920's and 1930's, emphasized that perception involved apprehension of the whole pattern of stimulation and they pointed to the primacy of the relations between elements in a visual stimulus. In Dunker's demonstration the spot is clearly at the focus of interest; it is the figure, and the screen is background. A movement altering the spatial relationship of figure to ground occurs when the screen moves. Clearly when we see something move relative to its background we interpret it as the thing itself moving against a stationary background, since we know that backgrounds do not make movements while foregrounds remain stationary.

The Gestalt, the whole visual scene in Dunker's demonstration, is clearly recognized as a figure (the spot) on a background, and it is this that gives rise to the illusion. The recognition of the relationship be-

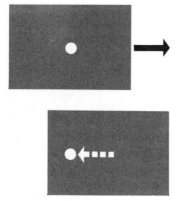

*Dunker's demonstration – though physically it is the screen that moves, perceptually it is the spot that is seen to move*

*Two shapes share a common border line, each competing with the other for attention. Depending upon the brain's decision as to which object is the figure and which the background, we see either a vase or two faces looking at each other*

tween figure and ground must precede the perception of the moving spot in this case, and we do not at present understand what kind of neural interconnection scheme organizes visual stimuli into figure-ground relationships.

The point is that although some relatively simple operations on the visual input are essential to the analysis of patterns of neural messages arising from the receptor surface, and though we may guess at the role and effects of the preliminary operations in perception, these operations are at most only the first stages. What I have described so far is the translation of patterns of receptor stimulation into the basic electrical terms in which the nervous system works, and then the translation of these signals into further codes reflecting specific aspects of stimulus patterns. The interpretation of this information as arising from objects in the outside world has yet to begin.

One of the few people who have used the widely accepted conclusions of Hubel and Wiesel as a basis for a more complete theory of pattern recognition, and tried to specify subsequent stages in the process, is N. S. Sutherland of the University of Sussex. He has set out some of the conditions that a theory of pattern recognition must fulfil, and has gone on to argue that detection of lines and edges is followed by sequences of logical operations which generate structural descriptions of the pattern. Structural descriptions specify not merely what lines and edges exist in the pattern but also what relationships exist between them. Thus the letter L might be specified as a vertical line joined at its bottom end to the left hand end of a shorter horizontal line. Neurally coded versions of such descriptions, rather than copies of retinal patterns, are stored, and whether we recognize a letter such as an L will depend on whether it fits a stored description. In this scheme several conditions for a pattern recognizing scheme are met. The stored description allows recognition of patterns independently of their size, position and colour; and Sutherland has gone on to show how elaborations of this scheme meet other conditions whereas alternative schemes will not.

Even this theory does not go nearly far enough, however. Perception also involves, amongst other things, the segmentation of very complex scenes into their component parts, and the interpretation of patterns as objects in the real world. We still understand very little about what operations the brain performs upon the input pattern to recognize objects. in the event of someone discovering a cell in the cat's cortex that did respond only to a visually presented mouse independently of size, colour, position and so on, then this finding would be of some mild interest, but we could not at present give any satisfactory account of the train of neuronal operations that had been performed by the cat's brain to classify that object, and to define 'mouseness'.

# SEEING IS BELIEVING 6

Kurt Koffka, in his famous book on Gestalt psychology, posed an important question: 'Do things look as they look because they are what they are?' Koffka's answer was no; otherwise we would not experience visual illusions, in which we simultaneously know that an object is of one kind but see it as something else. Perhaps then things look as they look because patterns of stimulation at the receptors are what they are. Again Koffka points out that this will not do. Some visual figures are ambiguous, and although producing the same pattern of retinal stimulation appear first as one thing, and then as another.

The Gestaltists emphasized the relationships within patterns: Gestalt means an organized whole in which each part affects every other. This principle they applied to perception, to answer the question of why things look as they look. They maintained that inside the brain neural processes reproduce the shape of the retinal image, and because of forces acting between neurones in the brain, parts of the pattern affect each other to organize the pattern of neural excitation into a whole that corresponds with perceptual experience. The forces, though they usually work to complete figures, and make them 'good', are occasionally responsible for creating illusions. The theory of forces in the brain has been shown to be wrong. It is in any case not an explanation to say that perceiving a pattern is brought about by reproducing its shape as a spatial distribution of neural activity in the brain. That merely

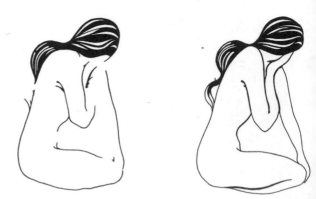

*Gerald Fisher's ambiguous figure. The centre picture is judged to be equally likely to appear as a man's face, or a girl kneeling; the drawings to left and right illustrate unambiguous versions of each subject*

postpones the problem of analysing spatial patterns from the retinal to the cortical stage.

Nonetheless Gestalt psychologists had hit upon an important problem, and discovered means for investigating it. They initiated an important direction of research in exposing ambiguities and studying illusions in perception. They pointed out that these were not just funny quirks and idiosyncrasies, but might give clues as to the essential nature of normal perception. The same mechanisms that enable us to see things correctly are also responsible for illusions.

Illusions and ambiguities perform a necessary function of 'making strange' the all-too-familiar processes of visual perception. Without this element of strangeness it may even be difficult to realize that there is anything to be understood in the process of seeing. However the strangeness of some features of perception gives us a lever to prise open the process a little, to catch perceptual mechanisms, as it were, unawares, and to glimpse some of the far from obvious principles underlying not only these stranger aspects of perception, but also its normal workings.

One such strange aspect was considered by Ludwig Wittgenstein, one of the greatest of modern philosophers. His discussion of perception is clearly influenced by the Gestaltists' investigations. Wittgenstein pointed out that in order to see an object in the world, we must see it as something. Indeed it is doubtful if we can ever see without 'seeing as'. Wittgenstein illustrated this by reference to an ambiguous figure, the duck-rabbit. You can see it as a picture of a duck or a rabbit, but not both simultaneously, nor as a random assemblage of lines. Simpler figures are even richer sources of ambiguity. A triangle can be seen as a geometrical diagram, as a triangular hole, or a triangular solid. It could be standing on its base or hanging from its apex. It could be a mountain, or an arrow head. It could even be an object that usually stands on end, but which has fallen over. With a little imagination (or help from an artist) you can see it now as this, now as that. The arrangement of three simple lines can take on a variety of significance. The variety exists because for any

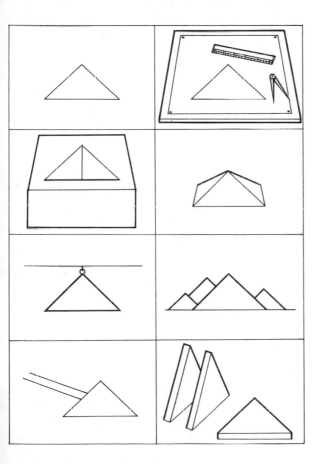

*Above: the duck-rabbit figure used by Wittgenstein to illustrate his discussion of perception. The probability of seeing either aspect is approximately equal, but, as with all ambiguous figures, it is only possible to perceive one interpretation at a time. Left: a very simple figure, for example, a triangle, can be interpreted in many ways*

*The Fraser spiral, one of the most powerful illusions known. The 'spiral' is in fact made up of concentric circles – clearly the figure does not look as it does because it is what it is*

interpretation there are no corroborative cues which confirm (or deny) the interpretation and stabilize it. When such cues are added, the percept immediately becomes stable.

How then must we understand perception? Firstly we must distinguish, as did the Gestalt psychologists, the different components of the perceptual process. First there is the distant stimulus, objects (such as tables and chairs) existing in the domain of the real world. An object reflects light some of which impinges on the retina. These patterns of light on the retina are not the distant object itself. They stand instead as tokens of that object; rather like money which in the way we behave towards it clearly betokens work, or a win on the football pools or goods from a shop. Money is not hours spent operating a lathe, or a coincidence of unpredictable events, or a washing machine, but it has a certain significance capable of relating our behaviour to these things. In the same way images on the retina betoken objects in the world, though obviously in a much more informative and complex way than money betokens work or goods. If interpreted properly, patterns impinging on the receptors allow the brain to know what the objects were from which those patterns arose. It is this interpretive process that constitutes seeing, and provides the basis for our perception of the same object despite the infinite variation (due to distance, position, etc.) of light patterns to which it can give rise.

The reason why perception is like it is seems clear; men (and other animals) were designed by their environment to live and act in that environment, and to manipulate it. One cannot direct actions towards patches of light or colour, only towards people, things and places. Perception therefore must be the business of interpreting patterns of receptor stimulation as objects, their attributes and their relationships; and creating in the mind of the perceiver, as a sort of model, the world towards which he directs his actions.

We can therefore distinguish not just the domain of objects in the external world (the distant stimulus), and the domain of patterns of receptor stimulation, but also the domain of percepts which are the creative interpretations of the mind, but which correspond more closely to the outside world than to the patterns of receptor stimulation.

When we try to understand perception from this point of view it is clear that there is no distinction between seeing something real and seeing a visual illusion. Reality and illusion are seen by the same perceptual processes. It is not the fact of illusions that should be regarded as odd. As Wittgenstein remarked, 'We find certain things about seeing puzzling because we do not find the whole business of seeing puzzling enough.'

## How is it possible?

The purpose of the rather lengthy prolegomena in this chapter is to make it clear that as well as involving classification of patterns (perhaps by means of structural descriptions) perception involves interpretation of the patterns as things in the real world. Indeed even

*Seen from one angle the Ames chair looks like a chair, from other angles it is seen to be what it is, a disjointed collection of rods and wires. Visual scenes may seem uniquely specified, but as far as retinal images are concerned they are infinitely ambiguous. Many different arrangements of objects could give rise to a particular retinal image*

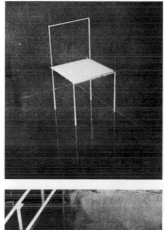

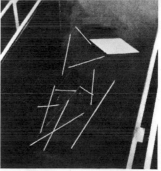

the simplest pattern classification processes do not proceed adequately unless elements and relationships in the domain of retinal stimulation are interpreted into things and their relationships in a self-consistent domain of objects. Even with the simple case of recognition of the letter L, lines are interpreted as the strokes that go to make up the letter. Thus our knowledge of objects, attributes and relationships that can exist in the object domain informs the perceptual processes as to how elements of the input pattern can be interpreted as particular parts of things, and the possible arrangements of objects that can occur in the real world inform the process as to which inter-relationships within the retinal stimuli are significant.

The question for those trying to understand the brain is 'How is all this possible?' In the first place what kinds of processes could conceivably be involved in achieving the interpretation, and in the second place how do the mechanisms of the brain actually carry out these processes?

One of several facts that points to perception being a construction (however vivid and convincing) is the flat two-dimensional structure of the retina in comparison with the patently solid appearance of things, and the evident existence of three dimensions in the visual space which we inhabit. At the very least this third dimension of visual space must be a construction. It does not exist as such on the retina.

Psychologists have expended a great deal of effort in trying to establish what information from the third dimension is available to an observer, and how it is used to build up a percept. It is, however, an over-simplification to suppose that this dimension is any more difficult to deal with than the other two. For in these as well, disjointed pieces of information from successive glances have to be interpreted to give the impression of a continuous visual scene.

If we consider the way an image is formed on the retina it is clear that for an object of a given size, the further away it is the smaller must be the retinal image. The size varies in an inverse relationship with distance;

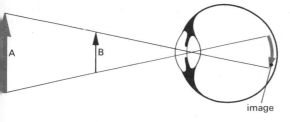

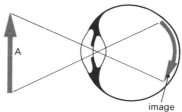
image                    image

wice the distance – half the size and so on. One can
lemonstrate an important psychological consequence
of this optical fact by creating an image on the retina
which stays the same size, and then looking at surfaces
t various distances. This can be done by producing an
fter-image, similar to the coloured after-image that
1as already been demonstrated on page 84.

For this demonstration stare at a lighted electric light
or about half a minute, looking fixedly at the same
pot. (The longest-lasting and most vivid after-images
re obtained following a period of a few minutes in
elatively dim illumination to allow the eyes to
ncrease their sensitivity.) After staring at the light
ulb, shut your eyes and you will see an after-image
of the same shape as the lamp. Now open your eyes
nd among the curious behaviour of such images you
vill notice that they move with the eye in the direction

*Arrow A is twice the size of B, but if it is at twice the distance from the eye A and B will produce identical retinal images. However, at the same distance as B, A would produce an image twice the size*

*Dürer's famous woodcut showing how the lute on the table will appear to the eye of the seated man. Perspective drawing is an attempt to reproduce retinal images on a flat surface – try tracing on a window with a felt pen the outline of objects seen through the window (as in Dürer's illustration)*

of gaze, and can therefore be 'projected' onto an surface. In a room in which the illumination is nc brighter than the lamp at which you stared, look at th opposite wall. The after-image will be projected ont it. Now look at a piece of paper held at arm's length Although the image certainly stays the same size o the retina, it changes its apparent size with distance being small when projected onto something close an large when projected onto something further away You can make precise measurements by projectin images onto a piece of paper at various distances an noting the apparent size of the image on the paper, an the distance of the paper from the eye.

As far as the geometry of visual image formatio goes, there is no way of telling whether an object suc as a stick is a big stick far away or a little one near b In other words, size on the retina alone does not allo\ us to know what size an object actually is, or determin what size we see it to be. The way in which the brai resolves the ambiguity of size and distance is by usin types of information (cues) available in the visuε scene to judge the distance of the object. Then with th retinal size and the distance known, the real size of th object is determined, and that is the size that we ten to see.

An experiment indicating this to be the case wa done by A. Holway and E. Boring. They sat observeι at the corner of two corridors that met at a right anglε In one corridor, ten feet away, was a screen on whic a round patch of light was projected. This patch wa the comparison stimulus and the subject could alter iι size. Down the other corridor was another scree which the experimenter moved to different distanc (ranging from 10 to 120 feet) from the observer. Afte each movement of this screen and before allowing th subject to view it, the experimenter adjusted the ligh patch so that its image always remained the same siz on the observer's retina, irrespective of the distanc for example, if he moved the screen to twice the di tance he had to double the actual size of the standar stimulus patch.

The subject's job was to adjust the comparison stimulus until it looked the same size as the standard. Under normal viewing conditions with both eyes, the subject was found to adjust the comparison stimulus until it was the same actual size (as measured with a ruler) as the standard at all distances: he saw the patch as the size it really was.

Then the observations were repeated with the subject using only one eye to view the stimulus, then with only one eye and viewing through a small fixed hole, and finally looking down a tunnel of black cloth which cut out almost all information arising from the visual context of the stimulus. Each of these steps reduced the information available to judge distance, and each reduced the tendency of the subjects to set the comparison stimulus to the same physical size as the standard. In the final condition their settings of the comparison patch remained almost constant with distance of the standard; just like the size of the image on the retina.

The demonstration with the after-images is an informal version of Holway and Boring's experiment: an image of fixed size on the retina is projected on surfaces at various distances. How far away we judge each surface to be determines how big the image looks.

*The retention of size constancy is not perfect. The far end of this building does look smaller than the near end, perhaps a quarter the size, but it does not look nearly as small as the retinal image might be expected to suggest. Try measuring the two ends and comparing their sizes*

*When objects such as the hand and the girl's face are nearly in line we can come closer to comparing their retinal sizes. Normally distance cues allow us to interpret objects as part of a three-dimensional scene so that they retain their proper sizes*

This of course is the inverse situation of the normal one. If someone walks towards us the size of the retinal image to which he gives rise enlarges, but instead of seeing the person growing from the size of Tom Thumb to a giant in a few steps we see a person of normal size coming nearer. This retention by objects of something close to their own characteristic size and shape, despite change in the retinal image, is known as constancy. Size constancy retention is not complete; things further away do look a bit smaller than they do when nearer, but not nearly as much smaller as the geometry of retinal images would suggest until they get so far away that distance becomes difficult to judge.

Constancy is obviously very useful since we act in a world of objects which generally maintain their size and shape. For some of our ability to judge distance, the brain must know this property of objects. Indeed this knowledge provides exactly the basis that is necessary for the brain to interpret changing retinal images as seen things in a three-dimensional world where objects have constant characteristics. In a science-fiction world where objects continually changed their size, shape, colour and brightness, we might experience 'a blooming buzzing confusion' just as we would if we actually experienced the disjointed and changing patterns on our retina.

One important matter that arises from this is the problem of what the cues are in the visual environment that allow us to judge the distance of objects. As well as the cues due to having two eyes, a series of experiments has identified many other important distance or depth cues: perspective, texture gradients, relative movements of objects as we move our head, shadows, colour and brightness differences, obscuration of one object by another, and the known sizes of objects, all provide powerful cues for the judgement of distance.

What we end up with as a visual percept is not a picture conforming to the geometrical optics of the eye, but an experience of ourselves inhabiting a visual space in which objects have their proper shapes, sizes and spatial relationships. Such a percept is clearly a construction produced by the brain; it does not correspond in any simple way to the patterns on the retina.

*A few of the cues to depth perception that allow us to judge distance. The left balloon looks closer because it is larger and brighter. Gradation of texture is a very powerful cue to depth, as is shadow. Notice that there are no lines that correspond to the outlines of the letters in this last example*

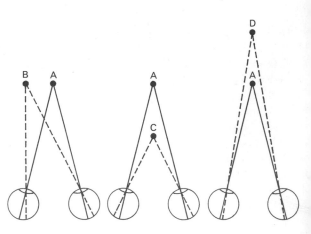

*Holding two pens or pencils up before the eye allows one to see the disparate locations of images on the retina. In the diagram A is the point fixated. B, about the same distance away as A, falls on corresponding points on the two eyes, but points nearer (C) and further (D) produce disparity, their images falling on non-corresponding areas of the retina*

## Stereoscopic vision

A major source of information about the third dimension comes from our having two eyes, each of which has a slightly different view of the world. Patterns of stimulation at the two eyes are brought together in the brain, and the fusion of the two slightly different images gives rise not to blurring, as one might suppose, but to a vivid impression of visual depth. The underlying mechanisms for this seem to be innate; and just as some people are genetically colour defective, some people do not have this binocular mechanism of depth perception.

The fact that you get a different view from each eye can easily be demonstrated by looking out of a window, with the line of sight passing close to the window frame. Now try alternately closing the left and right eye. That each eye has a different viewpoint is seen by the way in which the relationship between the window frame and outside objects jumps about as you do this.

To look more deeply into this matter, hold up in front of you two pencils, one at arm's length, and the other in line with it at about half the distance. Now look at (fixate) the further one and alternately close each eye. As the eyes are opened and closed the near pencil appears to jump back and forth: as the left eye opens the near pencil jumps to the right and *vice versa*. Next fixate the near pencil and again open and close the eyes alternately. Now the further pencil will jump to the left as the left eye opens. Lastly, bring the near pencil closer to you while continuing to fixate it, with both eyes, and you will see two images of the further pencil.

The explanation for these effects is that each point on the retina of one eye has a corresponding point on the retina of the other. When we fixate a thin vertical object such as a pencil the eyes swivel inwards so that each looks directly at it, and its image falls on corresponding points on both retinae. However, a diagram of the lines of sight to other objects nearer and further than the fixated pencil shows that images of these cannot simultaneously correspond in both eyes. This difference between these relative positions of the two images in the two eyes is known as disparity, and is seen in the jumping about of the non-fixated pencil when viewed with each eye alternately.

If the disparity becomes too large (as in the demonstration when the pencil close to the nose is fixated) double images of objects at other distances are formed. With smaller disparities only a single image is seen: fusion of the messages from both eyes occurs, and the disparity is interpreted not as two objects but as distance. Furthermore, the direction of the disparity (equivalent to whether the pencil not being fixated jumped towards the opening eye, or in the opposite direction) tells the brain whether objects are nearer or further than the fixation point.

The significance of disparity is exploited in the stereoscope invented in Victorian times by Wheatstone (who is also known for an electrical measuring circuit, the Wheatstone bridge). The instrument makes it possible to see two pictures taken from slightly different viewpoints separately with the two eyes, and to fuse them into a single visual image in which the features in the foreground stand out from those in the background. Apparently the stereoscope became widely used for pictures in which an important aspect was how some features of the female figure stood out, and with this usage it achieved a certain lack of respectability.

*The pictures in the margins on the next two pages can be viewed with a stereoscope made by taping two hand mirrors together and placing the book as shown here. You see the left picture with the left eye, and the right picture with the right eye and superimpose them. Be careful not to tilt the mirrors up or down. Overleaf, top: a simple 3-D stereoscopic diagram. Because the centre circle is relatively displaced in the two sides it is seen to be further away when the outer circles are fused. Centre: a Victorian stereoscopic subject. Bottom: a pair of Julesz figures in which a square in the centre appears nearer. (You have to be very careful to get this last pair in register)*

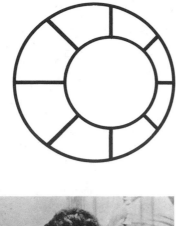

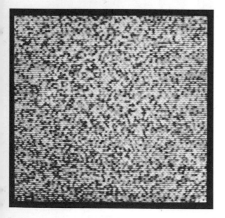

For those willing to suffer any social reproach that may still linger on, it is possible now to buy stereoscopes, with assorted views, and even stereoscopic cameras. Alternatively it is easy with two small mirrors to make a stereoscope, slightly modified from Wheatstone's design.

The definitive experiments isolating the aspect of the visual patterns that gives rise to stereoscopic depth was achieved rather recently by Bela Julesz. He used a computer to generate random dot patterns which could be viewed stereoscopically. There seems to be no difference between these patterns when viewed ordinarily. When viewed through a stereoscope and fused however, the particular pair of Julesz patterns shown here is seen to contain a central square, seen in depth. What Julesz has done is to shift the random pattern within that square a little to one side, thus creating disparity. When viewing Julesz patterns for the first time it often takes several minutes for the central square to be seen standing out from the picture. This itself is of interest; we have to register the disparity first in order to perceive the square shape, and this may be an unfamiliar sequence of operations. It may be more usual first to recognize an object, and then for disparity cues to enhance the depth effect.

It is now clear why two eyes are an advantage, and why most mammals bring fibres from corresponding points in each eye together in the brain. In the cat it has recently been shown that many of the cells which respond to lines and edges receive input from both eyes, and that each such cell responds best to a particular degree of retinal disparity. These cells seem to be selectively tuned to this pattern which gives information about the third dimension, and it is just such information which the brain needs to construct the visual world of objects in space which we see.

However, though the third dimension is more vivid when viewing with both eyes, the world does not suddenly collapse into a flat sheet when one eye is closed. Disparity is just one of the dozen or so types of information (cues) we use to construct visual depth.

any one of them will give an impression of distance, and since most visual situations abound with such cues one presumes that the brain admits all this information as evidence for the interpretations or hypotheses it makes.

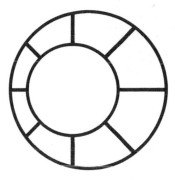

## Painting and seeing

It is not out of place when thinking about the task the brain undertakes in reconstructing our visual environment to consider how painters attempt to capture or create visual scenes.

The first thing a painter has to learn if he wants to paint a representational (i.e. realistic) picture of some scene, is to learn to stop seeing it in the way that he normally does, and the way most of us do all the time. For instance, when I look across the desk at which I am writing to the corner of the room I see a white wall and ceiling. The walls and ceiling are uniformly white, and the same white. They look that way, and indeed I know it to be true because I decorated the room myself. If I were to paint a picture of that corner though, I would have to paint the two walls and ceiling each in a different shade of grey in order to make it look (in the painting) like a corner of a room with walls and ceiling of the same colour.

A part of a representational painter's apprenticeship is to stop seeing objects, and to look for and represent patches of light, shade and colour. This does not mean that he has to start consulting his retinal images; it is doubtful whether we can ever do that. It does mean that he has to learn to see in a new and peculiar way.

The introduction of perspective into painting is a phase in the history of art known to everyone with any interest in painting, and is discussed, for instance, in E. H. Gombrich's famous book on the relationship of painting to the psychology of vision, *Art and Illusion*. The painters of the Renaissance had to learn not to see things (buildings, people and so on) in the way that they normally did, but to reproduce on canvas some of the properties of the retinal image; the diminution of size, the convergence of parallel lines, the increase

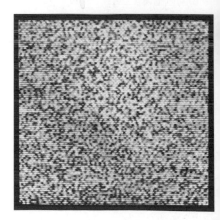

in density of elements in a textured surface, the increase of haziness and slight bluish tinge, which take place with increased distance from the observer. The technique of holding up the pencil before the eye to judge size is, for instance, an attempt to get away from the constancy mechanism. People looking at the picture then have the cues available to their own receptor processes so that they too can interpret them and see the scene that the artist had in mind.

Painting before the Renaissance is illustrative of processes of seeing in a quite different way. In such pictures the people depicted are all roughly the same size: that is the way people are, and that is the way we see them. Furthermore, there is usually no real attempt to represent anything in detail.

In the Bayeux Tapestry, all the people are much the same size. Kings are made easily recognizable, for instance, by a crown (worn frequently). Castles and other buildings are too small to contain the people on them or inside them. A hill held by the English in the battle is the same size as the soldiers on top of it. Yet none of these things matter. The figures look a bit quaint and funny to us, who are used to perspective drawing and photographs. But in a sense the mediaeval pictures tell us as much about perception as photographs.

In exactly the same way that different aspects of retinal images betoken aspects of objects in the world, the mediaeval artist used conventionalized figures to betoken people, ships, sovereignty and death. But the

*Above: trompe de l'oeil in the Palazzo Ducale, Urbino. The skilful panelling of this room creates an extraordinary effect of depth, although it is in fact quite flat. Opposite: this ceiling, painted by Pozzo in S. Ignazio, Rome, between 1691 and 1694, again is quite flat, but depth cues give a splendid impression of three dimensions, extending the architecture of the church towards the heavens. The style of the Bayeaux tapestry (below) is quite different from Renaissance painting. People and objects are represented schematically, regardless of their relative proportions, but in this forerunner of a strip cartoon cum propaganda document, the reality of the events depicted is no less striking*

figures are not so conventionalized as to be unrecognizable to the uninitiated. The way in which writing has developed from hieroglyphs did finally lead to altogether more arbitrary symbols. In mediaeval or ancient Egyptian pictures, however, the tokens are just sufficiently like the objects represented to be instantly recognizable, but usually not much more elaborate than necessary. By their positions and relationships one can see what the people depicted are doing, and a whole picture conveys meaningful information. Whereas Renaissance art was concerned with creating an illusion, pre-Renaissance art depicted reality; real people engaged in real transactions. By making explicit the symbolic nature of representation, it short-circuited the process of retinal images betokening things in a real world.

*In the development of writing, symbols became more and more arbitrary, and in Egyptian hieroglyphs one can follow this process. Here is an account of the life of a councillor, who is designated by his chain of office (an arched loop seen directly in front of the face of the largest picture of the man). It appears repeatedly in the text and various other characters (e.g. birds) are easily recognized*

In more modern times, as a result of painting having passed through these historical phases, painters know how to play one aspect of the visual process off against another, the powerful creation of illusion against the symbolic object, to produce visual puns. They also experiment with lines and patches of colour to see what impression these might give, and from some of the elements on which vision depends they can create entirely new worlds.

## Visual mechanisms

Some of this chapter has been devoted to exploring Wittgenstein's question, 'How is this possible?' I have mentioned a very few of the elements that make possible the perception of a real world 'out there', and sketched the role of distance cues in creation of the solid object in the mind of the observer. About the mechanisms that achieve it I have said little, and in fact little is known.

What we do know about are some of the preliminary operations performed on retinal patterns, detection of movement, collation of information from receptors to give a code interpretable as colour, detection of lines and edges, and measurement of retinal disparity. We may further suppose that these and other features of retinal patterns are incorporated into structural descriptions of a kind that allow interpretation of the retinal pattern into the domain of objects in a real world: our model of the world as it seems to be. Only at this last stage do patterns acquire any significance for perception or action.

Perhaps the main quality of behaviour which has seemed characteristic of life, and unlike anything expected of machines or mere puppets is its purposefulness. It was this quality which no doubt gave rise to the idea that life itself was something special, set apart from matter and machinery by a vital force. Indeed it has seemed until recently that to attribute purpose to any mechanical process involved an obvious contradiction. Any physical machine, the argument runs, must proceed from cause to effect. But purpose implies that some desired state of affairs in the future can affect events in the present, and this is patent nonsense. Therefore either there is some mysterious vital force attaching to life, and not to non-living processes, or living processes organized in terms of physics and chemistry cannot really be purposeful at all.

To some extent Darwin with his theory of natural selection sidesteps this dilemma. Since any form of life must be well fitted to the environment in order to have survived, any particular animal will clearly seem to an observer to be purpose built, and to behave in a purposeful way towards that environment. Darwin devoted a chapter of *The Origin of Species* to behaviour. Perhaps rather craftily he explained in the first paragraph of that chapter that he had nothing to say about how animals might be able to behave in the manner that they do. He then went on to demonstrate that patterns of purposeful behaviour could be accommodated by his theory, and that they were at least as

*Opposite: building a nest is evidently a very purposeful activity; we no longer need to appeal to vital forces to explain such behaviour*

important as bodily make-up for evolutionary success of a species.

Darwin called these patterns of behaviour, instincts. One cannot consider any animals in the range from insects to the higher mammals without being impressed both by the appropriateness of instinctive behaviour to the animal's way of life, and by the highly directed way in which goals seem to be sought and achieved. For instance, as Linnaeus pointed out, ants keep greenfly rather like cattle, apparently for the purpose of milking them of a sweet secretion which the ants eat. It is difficult to see a bird collecting twigs and straw without supposing that it is doing so in order to build a nest. The worst thing that we could think about our own behaviour, instinctive or otherwise, would be that it was purposeless. Indeed the great appeal of Freud and psychoanalysis is due to the idea that even irrational and insane behaviour is dependent upon strivings towards purposes and goals, but ones of which we are not directly aware.

How then, without resort to mystical forces, can purposeful behaviour be explained; how can the future control the present?

## Feedback and control systems

In retrospect the answer seems simple enough. If it were possible to define some desired state of affairs that might occur in the future, and to characterize or represent that state in the brain, then this symbolic representation of an idealised future in which purpose is attained (though not the future itself) could be used to direct behaviour.

It is in machines that this simple but powerful idea has had its main application. The result is automation, and automatic control is achieved by machines acting with a purpose. The idea is perhaps seen most clearly in a machine which stands astride the past (when most physical work was done with muscles) and the present (when almost none is). The machine is the windmill. Within one aspect, a mill provides power, to grind corn or pump water, but within another aspect there is

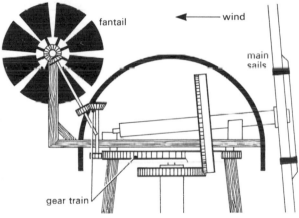

fantail

← wind

main sails

gear train

*The fantail mechanism that keeps the mill's main sails into the wind is one of the easiest control systems to understand, and it embodies important principles common to all regulatory devices*

the seed of the machine that deals not with power and work, but with information.

The informational aspect is exhibited in the fantail, which was patented by a man named Lee in England in 1745. The purpose of the fan at the back of the mill's cap is to keep the main sails facing the wind. This purpose is embodied in the fan by setting it at right angles to the main sails, so that should the wind start to blow from a new quarter it blows on the fan, rotating it in

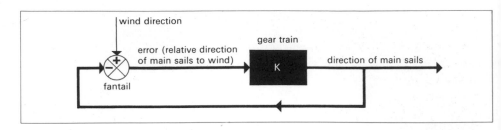

wind direction

error (relative direction
of main sails to wind)

gear train

K

direction of main sails

fantail

*The block diagram (part of the language of control theory) allows one to describe systems independently of the particular means by which information is carried. This diagram is for the fantail mechanism. The K within the box is a multiplying function and the sign X within the circle represents addition according to the signs written. Arrows represent signals, in this case various directions and gear rotations*

such a way as to drive a train of gears in the direction that will turn the cap of the mill until the wind no longer rotates the fan, and the main sails again face the wind. Expressed in other words, when the difference (or error) between the desired and actual direction of the wind reaches a certain value, the wind starts to turn the fantail so as to reduce this difference.

Measurement of an actual state of affairs, feeding back this information, and comparing it with a desired state is the essence of the automatic control system employed in the fantail mechanism.

The fundamental structure of such systems is drawn in diagrams which do not necessarily specify whether the information is carried in the rotation of a gear train as in the windmill, in the movements of a series of levers as in Watt's famous steam-engine governor, or, as is by far the most common today, by electronic means. Information is essentially independent of the medium in which it is carried, and it is this fact that allows the same fundamental control system to be constructed out of cogwheels or transistors. More importantly, it is the possibility of representing information in different physical systems that makes purposive machines possible at all, since they need to represent within their own workings a state of affairs that occurs in the external world. The significance of this fact extends yet further, for embodiment of information in different forms underlies the capacity of our own brain to understand anything at all. When we comprehend some aspect of the workings of the physical world we reconstruct the information in a symbolic structure (presumably embodied in neuronal circuits) within the brain. A correct representation, the parts and interactions of which we can describe to ourselves or others, constitutes the understanding.

In the problem of purposive behaviour (in which the future must be symbolically represented) we again appreciate the power of Craik's proposal (introduced in Chapter 1) that the brain must be able to act as a model of the world. How does the idea work in practice when we try to explain particular pieces of behaviour?

## Homeostasis

Purposive regulation in biology has come to be named homeostasis. The term expresses the fact that many of the processes of life are regulated; they are maintained with great tenacity, despite disturbing influences which tend to divert them from their course. Thus body temperature, the concentration of the blood, the amount of oxygen being supplied to the cells, and many other bodily variables are regulated by control systems that are closely related to the ones that keep the windmill sails into the wind, or steam engines running at a constant speed despite large variations in external conditions.

About thirty years ago, the very general nature of such systems began to be recognized and the term 'cybernetics' was coined by Norbert Wiener to designate the theory of control and communication within animals and machines. At very least any control system needs to have means for representing a desired state and for detecting deviation of the actual conditions from it, means for feeding back the information derived from this measurement, and with the use of some externally derived energy, the means for using this information to direct the system in such a way as to reduce the discrepancy.

## Motivated behaviour

Control theory has now become sophisticated: it allows rockets to be guided automatically (towards planets or cities), industrial plants to be regulated, and many physiological processes of the body to be understood. At about the time that the theory of control was beginning to be formulated, it was also recognized that it applied not only to bodily processes and automated machinery, but equally to the way in which the brain produces behaviour.

Part of the vast problem of how patterns of movement appropriate to achieve some end are produced, independently of starting position, or of the position of objects towards which these actions are directed, or of events which tend to divert movements from their course, can be tackled using the principles of control theory. These ideas are also applicable to some whole sequences of behaviour in which purposeful progress is made towards some desired state or goal, be it simply to feel warm, dry, well fed and comfortable, or to write a great masterpiece.

C. L. Hull was one of the first to exploit these ideas in this context. He supposed that hunger, or other departures of bodily processes from their ideal state, were needs which were detected by the brain. Needs induced drive, which was the energy that impelled behaviour without giving it direction, somewhat after the fashion of the engine in a motor car. Under the influence of drive the animal would wander around, and perform various behavioural patterns (responses) until by chance one of them was followed by finding and eating some food which in turn brought about reduction in the need, turning off the drive and stopping behaviour. Hull went on to study how direction was imposed on behaviour by learning, which he supposed to be the retention for future re-enactment of those responses which had previously led to the reduction of drive.

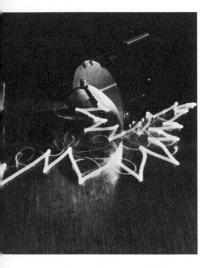

*A mechanical tortoise which has an element of purpose. It is equipped with a photoreceptor and a touch-detector, and is programmed to avoid objects it bumps into and to approach moderately bright lights. Its behaviour as seen in this timelapse photograph is not unlike that of paramecia (see page 14)*

Though simple, and as some of the many hundreds of experiments performed to test Hull's theories have shown, in some major respects mistaken, this theory was a landmark. It represents one of the first hypotheses of how purposive behaviour might be achieved and what the essentials of a complete behaving organism might be. When mechanical models were made to embody this kind of theory, these were the first

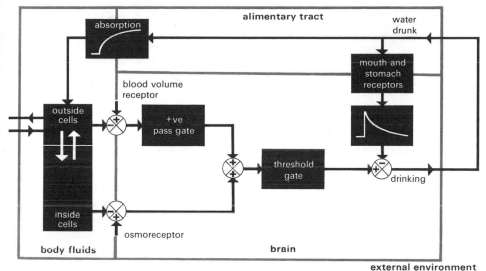

The following labels appear in the diagram:

alimentary tract

water drunk

absorption

mouth and stomach receptors

blood volume receptor

outside cells

+ve pass gate

threshold gate

inside cells

drinking

osmoreceptor

body fluids

brain

external environment

*The system which controls a rat's body fluids has been simulated in a computer, and the diagram above illustrates a small part of the program and shows the feedback loop concerned with drinking*

artefacts that did seem to behave in a purposeful way that could easily be mistaken for that of an animal. The idea of the animal as a control system also allows us to see that a role of receptors is to act as measuring instruments, detecting deviations of their surroundings from a representation of the desired state.

A number of processes of animal motivation have been analysed in terms of their roots in control systems that regulate bodily process. The mechanism of thirst is one of the best understood examples. In order to control drinking, the brain has first to measure the deviations from an ideal state of the available water in the body. This control is of the first importance for living things, as 60 to 70 per cent of the body is water. About two thirds of the body's water is contained within the cells, and the rest is made up of fluid (such as the blood) which surrounds the cells. In order to get a reasonable estimate of the state of the body water, the brain therefore makes two measurements, one of the amount of water within cells, and the other of the amount of water outside them. For each measurement there is a special receptor system. The information from the two sets of receptors is added together and generates 'thirsty behaviour'.

water drunk (ml)

10

5

0

50    100
minutes

*Above: a comparison between the rat's drinking response (dotted line) when injected with salt directly into a vein (below) and the ouput of the computer simulation (solid line)*

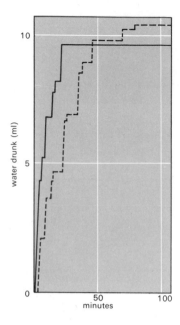

This simple system however needs to be made more complex, because the time taken for the water to get from the stomach into the blood and into the cells where it could be measured by the receptors that initiated the thirst would cause difficulties. The animal would go on drinking for long after he had swallowed enough water to repair the initial need.

To solve this problem the system also measures the amount of water passing through the mouth, and contained in the stomach, subtracting the estimate of the quantity drunk from the estimate of water needs. Firm experimental evidence for such operations has been found. But here another problem arises. What happens to the measurement of water passing through the mouth? If this signal were permanently subtracted from the measurement of need, then the next time a water deficit occurred, the estimate would be too small because of this quantity which had been subtracted from it. Clearly the signal measuring the water passing through the mouth must die away, and here arises the need for another representational process. If the rate of dying away of this signal reproduced exactly the rate of absorption of the water into the blood, then the animal would drink neither too much nor too little, and this is the present hypothesis about the measurement of water passing through the mouth.

The foregoing gives some idea about the kind of thing involved in working out the basis of straightforward behaviour like drinking. In fact a computer simulation which represents thirst and the control of body water is much more complex than this. It does however lead to the satisfying result of having a relatively complete and convincing explanation of an aspect of behaviour. Because it exists as a working model in a computer program, the theory is quite explicit in its predictions, so that it can be rigorously tested and modified where simulation and experiment fail to match.

Unfortunately as far as explaining all motivated behaviour of animals, the theory of simple control systems is not enough, and wider understanding of how

*A sexual display by a male Argus pheasant – one of the illustrations from Darwin's book The Descent of Man. This instinctive behaviour is dependent on hormones and an appropriate partner*

models behave purposefully is needed. For instance, in sexual behaviour there is no bodily quantity that is regulated. Instead sex depends largely on sensory signals from outside the body and upon hormonal signals from within.

Sexual displays and courtship rituals enable animals to choose a suitable mate. Only the right patterns of movement, plumage and so forth are recognized as indicating a receptive partner of the same species and opposite sex, and the patterns conforming to each animal's representation of a mate are precisely those which prepare for and initiate sexual activity. These signals in many animals are only effective if a certain hormonal state exists. Hormonal signals serve to induce sexual behaviour at appropriate times; initiating it to start with in animals that are sufficiently mature to care for offspring. Then, in many animals, hormonal signals induce mating only at certain seasons, and thus arrange sexual activity suitably in advance of the best period of the year for rearing young. These hormonal timing mechanisms model the alternation of the seasons: animals do not merely respond to good weather, they anticipate that Spring will come.

Internal timing is also crucial for the behaviour of sleeping and waking. Some animals such as bats and moles operate well only in darkness. Others depending heavily on vision, go about their business during the light. Alternation of sleep and wakefulness thus corresponds with the alternation of animals' preferred phases of activity. One might argue that all that any animal needed to do in order to organize its life appropriately would be to have some light-detector that induced activity appropriately during either darkness or light. But such a scheme will not do: an animal at the bottom of a dark hole would never know that daylight had come. What is needed is a model that reflects the alternation of light and darkness, and allows

*Artificial clocks and biological clocks are models of the earth's rotation. This one at Hampton Court is very explicit in its representation of astronomical cycles, and shows phases of the moon and signs of the Zodiac as well as time of day*

the animal to keep in time with the world without being totally dependent on it.

Thus sleep depends largely upon an internal rhythm, which periodically produces activity and inactivity. The reason why man now spends a third of his life in apparently useless inactivity may simply be that during evolution this was the biological answer to how to keep still and quiet so as to avoid predators in disadvantageous lighting conditions. Maybe man has inherited this pattern although since the invention of electric lighting, he no longer needs it. In another sense we can all testify to the fact that we do need sleep, and those who have flown the Atlantic can also testify to the fact that their own internal clocks have an existence of their own and take some time to resynchronize with a daytime period several hours out of time with the previous one.

Sleeping (and many other behavioural and physiological processes) are partly dependent on internal clocks which model the rotation of the earth, but the matter is not as simple as this. There is not just one type of sleep, but two, which alternate throughout the sleeping period. In one state the brain adopts patterns of electrical activity that are very different from those of wakefulness, but in the other, although the person is just as fast asleep, with his eyes shut and unaware of what is going on around him, the electrical activity of the brain becomes similar to the pattern during wakefulness. What is more, if a person is aroused during one of these periods of so-called paradoxical sleep, he almost invariably reports that he has just been dreaming, an infrequent result if he is wakened from the other phase of sleep. Possibly the reason for this dream phase of sleep, is that deprived of external events the brain needs to supply some simulated visual, auditory and other stimuli (hallucinations) of its own in order to keep nerve networks properly adjusted. It is known that individual nerve cells deprived of stimulation alter their threshold properties. Maybe animals having solved during evolution the problem of remaining inactive and without boredom during

*Small metal discs taped on to the head record averaged electrical activity of millions of neurones (electroencephalography), the output from each disc being traced on the moving strip of paper in the foreground. Below: four traces showing records while awake and alert (1), relaxed with eyes closed (2), and asleep (3 and 4). Notice the progressive increase in size and decreasing frequency of the waves, but in (4) the EEG looks similar to the waking state though the subject is asleep – and probably dreaming*

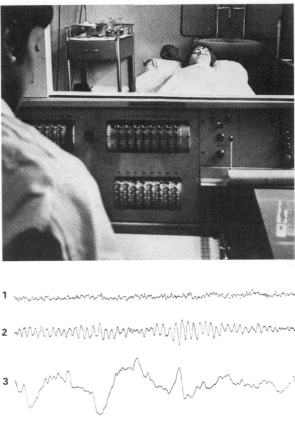

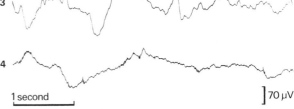

1 second   ] 70 μV

their disadvantaged phase, had also to solve the problem of stopping the brain from getting out of adjustment.

At all events it is clear from the few systems of motivation that have been mentioned that purposive behaviour depends upon the brain operating with models of the outside world. Thirst depends partly on a model of an ideal state, sex on representations of adequate sexual partners, and both sex and sleep on biological clocks which model periodic changes in the environment. Each system is capable of initiating and stopping the appropriate behaviour. But though for instance a homeostatic system of thirst explains the control of a single variable such as drinking, it does not explain how appropriate patterns of behaviour are contrived or directed when more than a single choice from two alternatives (such as drinking or not drinking) or the control of a single variable is involved. When there are more than two possibilities to choose from none of the mechanisms discussed will specify the direction to choose. In many kinds of situation however, men and animals habitually choose actions from a large number of possibilities.

## Specific patterns of motivated behaviour

At present we know very little about the mechanisms that make such complex choices and organize apt patterns of motivated behaviour, except that such mechanisms exist, and that they seem to depend upon complex innate structures within the brain.

The instincts of which Darwin wrote, and which have fascinated naturalists for many years, are examples of specific patterns of motivated behaviour. Each species has its own characteristic way of eating, moving, hunting, fighting, fleeing from attack, courting, mating and so on. Each of these patterns is closely adpated to the objects and events to which it is directed.

The fact that such patterns are so characteristic of the species is *prima facie* evidence of their innate character. Furthermore without a very extensive, genetically determined repertoire of such behaviour patterns, no animal would survive for more than a few days. If Hull were really correct in supposing that motivation merely energized behaviour, without giving it direction, almost no animals in the wild would ever survive. Cats, for instance, do not need to be taught the strategies necessary to catch mice or birds: the stealth and cunning with which they sit silently hidden in appropriate places ready to pounce is innate. In self defence nearly every animal when

*The innate stealth of the hunting cat*

frightened becomes motionless. It does not have to learn that its predators detect movement more easily than any other visual stimulus. These pieces of knowledge incorporated into instinctive mechanisms are part of the inheritance of the species.

None of this contradicts the evidence that learning affects both the tendency of instinctive behaviour patterns to appear, and the skill with which they are performed. The point is that if learning were all that the animal had to guide his behaviour then he would be unlikely to survive: what the animal does learn is closely dependent on rather specific innate mechanisms. The existence of patterns of organization underlying these types of behaviour has been demonstrated in a striking way.

Many years before Penfield had elicited fragmentary sensations and motor movements from his neurological patients by electrical stimulation of the cortex, W. R. Hess in Zurich had shown that similar stimulation of regions beneath the cortex in animals gave rise to integrated patterns of motivated behaviour. Hess experimented principally with the elicitation of rage behaviour, in which when the electrical stimulation began, animals would assume an aggressive posture and then launch a properly directed attack at an object that would not normally disturb them at all. Presumably the neural organization that controls this behaviour has such well developed interconnections that passing electrical current among the neurones sets up, by virtue of these connections, the patterns of nerve impulses that normally generate rage behaviour. Though it is the object being attacked that guides the direction of the aggression, it is the electrical stimulation that seems to be responsible for eliciting from an innate organization the ordered pattern of behaviour that the particular species of animal normally uses for purposes of attack.

The innateness of such behaviour patterns has subsequently been demonstrated by showing that electrical stimulation of the brains of cats that had been raised in isolation from other cats can induce them to kill rats. Furthermore, the movements and strategies that they used were no different from those used by cats reared in the usual way.

The implantation of electrodes in order to control behaviour has become a common experimental technique. Under an anaesthetic, the head of an animal (most often a rat) is located in a frame, so that the skull is fixed in a known position with reference to that frame. A special atlas of the brain, known as a stereotaxic atlas, is used to define the point to which the tip of a thin wire electrode will be directed through a small hole in the skull. After implantation the electrode is provided with a small socket via which electrical stimulation can be applied. Then the whole assembly is cemented to the skull.

Animals quickly recover from this operation and live quite happily with their permanent electrode assembly in place, apparently unaware of it. To perform an experiment, thin flexible wires are plugged into the assembly, and so long as they are suspended up and out of the way, animals are not troubled by them. For stimulating animals wandering in a large space, radio techniques can be used to substitute for wires.

Among the specific behaviour patterns that have been evoked by electrical stimulation at different sites in the brain are eating, drinking and fighting. It has also been found that, as well as electrodes, tiny steel tubes (made from small-diameter hypodermic needles) can be implanted into the brain. Into these can be

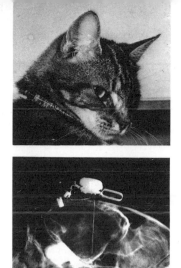

*Electrodes can be fitted with miniature radio receivers so that stimulation from a distance is possible without the necessity for long leads. Above: the X-ray shows the receiver and electrode in place, the assembly being scarcely visible as a small bump beneath the fur on the cat's head. Below left: a bull fitted with radio-controlled electrodes in the act of charging. On stimulation he comes skidding to a halt (right), but does this help us to understand the nature of the mechanisms underlying aggression?*

*An alternative method of brain stimulation involves injection of small quantities of chemicals. Here a satiated rat is induced to eat by the injection of a transmitter nor-adrenalin into the hypothalamic region of the brain*

*Drugs that act on the brain have specific mental and behavioural effects largely because they differentially affect various transmitters. Here are the progressive effects of a dose of LSD on an artist's drawing of himself*

injected minute quantities of chemicals such as transmitter substances and hormones. As might be expected from the nature of neural transmission, these too are capable of stimulating nerve cells that are near the tip of the tube, and of evoking specific patterns of behaviour that depend upon the area of the brain, and upon the substance injected. As well as hungry and thirsty behaviour, sexual and maternal behaviour have been evoked by this direct chemical stimulation.

It is now well established that many of the different systems within the brain, and particularly those that are concerned with motivational and emotional behaviour employ different combinations of chemical transmitter substances (although any one will only cause either excitation or inhibition). It is, however, the multiplicity of chemical messengers used by the brain that allows drugs, ranging from aspirin to LSD to act differently upon the nervous system even when they are taken by the blood supply non-specifically to all parts of the brain. In particular the chemotherapy used in many kinds of mental illness depends upon this fortunate arrangement whereby different systems seem to use different transmitter substances, when logically only two, one excitatory and one inhibitory, would do.

Perhaps most remarkable of all experiments on direct stimulation of the brain, electrical stimulation applied to some areas can serve as a reward. Perhaps the

*Electrical stimulation sometimes acts as a reward and self-stimulation has been observed in many of the species used in research. Here a crocodile – an unusual experimental animal – swims between two plates to receive stimulation*

effective areas are those involved in signalling that a desired state (such as is represented in a control system) is being approached. At any rate, animals will press a small lever to switch on electric current to certain parts of the brain. With some electrode placements they press the lever continually, day in and day out, even completely neglecting food and water. This so-called self-stimulation seems to be a powerful reward which is never satiating. It conforms even more closely to Oscar Wilde's 'most perfect type of perfect pleasure' than the cigarette to which he originally applied the epigram. 'It is exquisite and it leaves one unsatisfied. What more can one want?'

Though initially performed only in animals, the implantation of self-stimulation electrodes has been extended even to a few human psychiatric patients who apparently find the stimulation pleasurable. It is interesting that these experiments on people, ac-companied by the usual rather lame justifications, have not really added to our understanding. No doubt, however, this sort of thing will spread, and in due course we may expect to hear how the delightful ex-periences to be gained with psychoactive drugs pale into insignificance beside the joys (not to mention the cosmic insights) derived from electrical stimulation of the brain.

What has been shown by the results of electrical and chemical stimulation, and from parallel experiments in which small areas of the brain are removed, is something of the position and extent of the parts of the brain concerned with patterns of motivated and emotional behaviour. These experiments also indicate that motivated behaviour involves not so much trial and error progress towards a goal, as well-defined strategies to achieve particular ends, and that these strategies depend on neural organizations that have a substantial innate basis. It is however a mistake to suppose that these experiments reveal much about the nature of the neural organization that generate the behaviour.

In order to understand this organization we need to discover principles (perhaps within the context of control systems) that define how choice is made from many alternative paths that might lead to a goal, and how actions and intentions are translated into detailed sequences of muscle movements. At the moment we do not have much idea of how these things could conceivably be done: discovery of principles at least as powerful as feedback and the representation of desired states may be needed before we do. Such principles are unlikely to be revealed in the course of prodding into

*Bizarre behaviour – such as gnawing at a screwdriver – is sometimes produced by stimulating the brain. It is questionable whether these odd effects help us to understand normal behaviour any more than inserting a high-voltage probe into a computer is likely to be the best way of finding out how it works*

the brain substance, any more than we would be likely to discover how a computer program worked by examining the machine's behaviour following largely blindfold insertions of long poles carrying high voltage into its centre, or after exploding small bombs inside it. Various kinds of behaviour might result, some of it bizarre, some well organized. Some aspects of the behaviour might show that the computer had a well-defined internal organization, but it is doubtful whether it could ever tell us what the organization was or how the machine solved differential equations.

Instead, more subtle tactics need to be employed. Behaviour must be studied with a view to finding out what kinds of internal organization are consistent with it, in the sense that the organization of feedback control is consistent with the rudiments of purposive behaviour, and in the sense that a certain kind of organization simulated by a computer program is compatible with some of the basic facts of thirst behaviour. Once theories consistent with behaviour have been invented (it is not easy to see that any other word than 'invented' is more appropriate), then we begin to use the knowledge gained from direct stimulation, lesioning and recording in particular parts of the brain to tell us where to look in order to try and find out how these principles are translated into neural practice. It may be possible to proceed in the other direction, from specific nerve cells and networks to general principles of brain organization, but it is not easy to see how.

Pieces of machinery made up of cogwheels and levers, of which the windmill is a splendid example, are probably the only kinds of mechanism that can be understood just by looking, aided with a push here and a pull there. Almost certainly it is a mistake to suppose that the brain will be understood simply by opening it up to look and prod inside it. We need to have some understanding of its principles of organization before we can correctly interpret what we find, or correctly understand how the machinery of the brain works to produce behaviour.

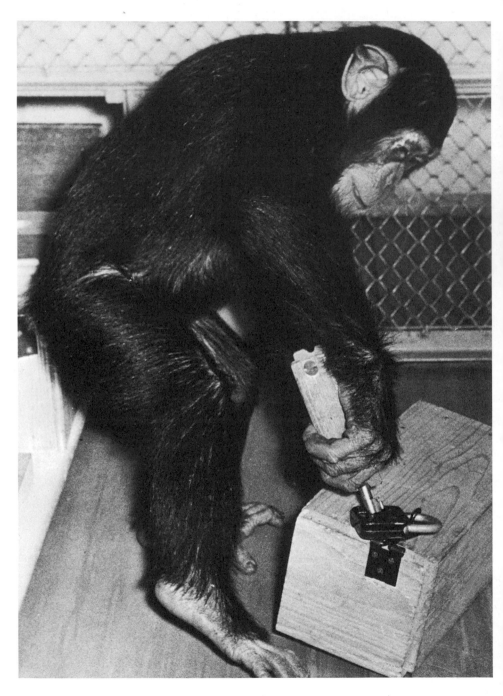

# LEARNING AND MEMORY

Learning and memory have fascinated psychologists and physiologists perhaps more than any other problem. Man's ability to benefit from personal and cultural experience is prized almost as much as his creativeness. At first sight, nothing seems more central to the adaptive success of those highest products of evolution, the mammals, than their capacity to learn.

If we want to understand learning we need first to find out what is learned in various kinds of situations. It also seems reasonable to start with learning in animals, for the brain processes of man are evolved from those of animals no less than are anatomical features. If we can understand simple cases of learning, then we may be better equipped to comprehend more complex varieties. This, and the fact that it is possible to perform physiological experiments on animals, is the reason why the interest of many who have tried to understand learning has been directed towards animals. So enthusiastic has the study of animal learning been at times that the rat has been referred to as 'a furry, white test-tube', and the conviction of some psychologists was that all the important problems in psychology could be attacked by studying a rat's behaviour at the choice point of a maze.

Today the more grandiose claims of the past seem absurd, yet they reflect a mood of the 1920's and 1930's in which the fruits of the scientific study of behaviour were beginning to be harvested. Nevertheless, the

*Opposite: the ability of animals to learn and solve problems seems similar to man's, but may be simpler for us to understand*

study of animal learning has brought many general insights into the process of learning in man, and besides that, animal behaviour is itself a subject of considerable fascination.

## The conditioned reflex

The most important figure in animal psychology then and now was I. P. Pavlov. He had already been awarded the Nobel Prize for his work on digestive physiology before he discovered and began to study the conditioned reflex. In the same way that the Sherringtonian reflex seemed to be the building block for the organization of the spinal cord, the Pavlovian conditioned reflex came to be regarded by many as the basis for the organization of the higher processes of the brain.

Typically in his experiments Pavlov used dogs on which a minor operation of transferring the opening of a salivary gland from inside the mouth to the skin on the outside surface of the cheek had been performed, so that the saliva could easily be collected and measured. Saliva was regularly produced almost immediately on placing food in a dog's mouth. This is an unlearned

*Pavlov (bearded), pictured here with his colleagues and an experimental dog, performed a series of classical experiments discovering and investigating the conditioned reflex – a learned response to a stimulus previously of no significance*

reflex, similar in character to withdrawing the hand from a flame. When a neutral stimulus such as the ticking of a metronome was introduced, it at first produced investigatory responses in which the dog turned its head towards it, but no saliva. If, however, the ticking sound were closely followed by the arrival of food in the dog's mouth on a number of occasions (trials) the saliva came to be secreted in response to the ticking even on a trial in which food was not placed in the mouth.

Pavlov regarded this result quite straightforwardly as being due to the formation of new neural connections in the brain. In an ordinary unlearned reflex, innate connections allowed environmental cause to determine a behavioural effect. In the conditioned reflex, new connections by way of which the environment could evoke behaviour were forged, in a manner that was determined by individual experience. Pavlov's claim was that this finding put the study of all higher nervous activity on an objective footing.

Pavlov's discovery and his theory of conditioned reflexes were influential in establishing the view that not just nerve cells, but behaviour and mental processes could be studied scientifically and finally understood. In advocating this view Pavlov encountered a certain amount of opposition. 'Your conditioned reflexes will hardly be popular in England, since they have a materialistic flavour' is what Pavlov remembers Sherrington to have said to him in London in 1912. A later Russian editor of Pavlov's works, explaining that Pavlov 'encountered the animosity of a number of scientists and idealist philosophers, lackeys of the imperialist bourgeoisie', seems to take a similar view to Sherrington, though he expresses it differently.

## Instrumental learning and behaviourism

At the turn of this century when Pavlov was discovering the laws of conditioning (now usually called classical conditioning), E. L. Thorndike in America was also experimenting on learning. He constructed boxes in which the door could be operated by an animal inside it, by, for instance, pulling a cord or pushing up a latch. Cats put inside these puzzle boxes before their daily feeding session learned, as Thorndike said, by trial and error, to open the door. The success that accompanied the correct manipulation apparently 'stamped in' the movements that were effective, so that they were learned, and were more readily repeated on each subsequent trial. On the basis of this, Thorndike enunciated the law of effect; a successful effect or result of an action leads to it being learned.

In Pavlovian conditioning, the experimenter repeats the sequence 'metronome ticking followed by food', so that the metronome comes to signal the arrival of food, but the dog's response of salivation has no influence on this event. In the form of learning which Thorndike investigated which came to be known as instrumental learning, the animal's action was instrumental in producing the food.

In the United States it was upon instrumental learning that concentration was the greatest. Behaviourism sprang from its early study and implied, amongst other things, the reduction of many psychological problems to understanding how appropriate behaviour could be learned, and thus of how to apply appropriate situations to produce learning. J. B. Watson, the founder of this view, was able confidently to write, 'There is no such thing as an inheritance of capacity, talent, temperament, mental constitution and characteristics. Give me a dozen healthy infants well formed, and my own specified world to bring them up in and I'll guarantee to take any one at random and train him to become any type of specialist I might select, doctor, lawyer, merchant-chief, and yes, even beggar-man and thief.'

The best known modern representative of behaviourism is B. F. Skinner. He rejects the problems of explaining how the brain works in order to concentrate upon finding out how best to modify and control behaviour by learning. Instead of speaking of the 'law of effect' Skinner uses the term 'reinforcement', which is anything that alters the probability of a response. It

is indeed the effect to which the law of effect refers, and may be food or some other reward. It may be something painful such as an electric shock, in which case the behaviour that is acquired is avoidance. Skinner claims, however, that punishment is less effective in behavioural control than positive (rewarding) reinforcement.

Skinner introduced a useful experimental arrangement whereby an animal in a special cage (Skinner box) was made responsible for feeding itself by pressing a lever to operate a switch. The rate of responding could be recorded, and the relationship of the responses to the delivery to the animal of a small quantity of food (a reinforcement) could be specified by apparatus consisting of electro-mechanical switches, counters and clocks.

Schedules of reinforcement could be arranged, for instance, to reward the animal after each response, after each second response, each tenth response or whatever the experimenter chose. In some schedules, the reinforcement was produced by the first response after a given fixed or variable time interval, and so forth. Skinner pointed out that each type of schedule

*Automatic apparatus for investigating animal behaviour was introduced by Skinner. This rat (left) has two levers to press and two stimuli to discriminate. Behavioural experiments of all kinds can be programmed and recorded with the type of equipment shown above*

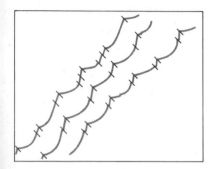

*Three cumulative records of behaviour: the slope of each curve represents rate of response and the short cross lines mark rewards. Here three animals worked alternately on a schedule with a fixed number of responses required for a reward (steep part) and a fixed interval before the next reward (scalloped part). Skinner claims that the schedules determine the performance and that the three animals, pigeon, rat and monkey, cannot be distinguished from these records*

produced a distinctive pattern of behaviour, and that in order to produce high sustained rates of responding, schedules where either a randomly varying number of responses was needed to earn the reward, or where it was delivered for the first response after a randomly varying time interval, were very efficient.

This principle has for long been exploited by gambling situations, in which the well trained gambler is difficult to distract, responds continuously often at a high rate, and is given reinforcements infrequently after some random and unpredictable amount of time or number of responses. The one-armed bandit is the gambling device most stripped of inessentials, and by means of it human behaviour can be brought under tight control, and no cage is needed.

## Generalization and discrimination

Both classical and instrumental methods have been important in more academic aspects of brain research, since with these methods the problems of what was learned and how it was learned could be tackled.

In Pavlov's laboratory it was shown that if a dog was conditioned to one stimulus, say, a musical tone at a certain pitch, then it would also respond, though not quite so vigorously, to a tone sounded at a slightly different pitch. The effect diminished as the stimulus was made more unlike that originally used for establishing the reflex. This phenomenon of generalization was also found to occur with instrumental learning. It is presumably of great value for animals living in a world where the same object shows similar but not identical aspects on different occasions.

Equally crucial is the phenomenon of discrimination. Pavlov discovered that although initial trials with stimuli similar to, but not identical with, the training stimulus were effective in eliciting the reflex, when these stimuli were shown repeatedly, but never accompanied by food, they ceased to produce saliva. The animal had clearly learned to associate one stimulus with food and the other not. In this way dogs were taught to discriminate squares from circles, clockwise

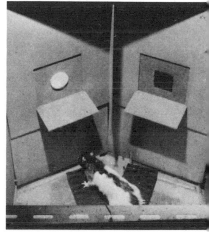

from anti-clockwise rotation of a disc, musical notes, and many other stimuli.

Instrumental learning has also been used to study discrimination. Indeed, so sophisticated have behavioural techniques now become that it is possible to train an animal by classical or instrumental methods and ask it, in effect, any question of the kind, 'Can you detect this stimulus or not?', 'Can you tell that this pattern is different from that?', 'Can you remember this event?' Almost any experimental task (not involving language) which one might put to a human subject can, by the use of behavioural techniques, be translated into a question that an animal can answer. In the last fifty years we have gathered an enormous amount of knowledge about the abilities of animals; whether they can see colour, what patterns they can recognize, which things they see as similar and which as different, how well they can hear, what kinds of things they can remember, and so forth.

*Above: the Lashley jumping stand, used for studying discrimination in the rat. The animal jumps towards one of the doors, and the one which is correct falls, giving access to food. Left: discrimination learning in the octopus: the animal lurks behind a stone but can be trained to emerge and approach particular shapes by rewarding it with a crab*

## Extensions of learning theory

One important result of understanding learning might be an increase in our ability to treat certain types of mental illness, particularly neuroses, which seem at least partly to arise from acquiring maladaptive behaviour patterns in learning situations.

Pavlov described what happened to some animals in experiments where a discrimination task was made too difficult. A dog undergoing training to discriminate circles from ellipses was first conditioned to respond with saliva to the circle. Then gradually ellipses more closely approaching the circle were shown, and never followed by food. But as the ratio of long to short axes of the ellipse reached 9:8, the discrimination failed to improve, and the animal instead of standing quietly and contentedly in the apparatus as was usual, began to squeal and struggle. It bit through and tore bits of the apparatus in the experimental chamber. On the next occasion when it was taken to the experimental room it barked violently and was reluctant to enter: in short, it showed all the symptoms of an acute nervous breakdown.

Pavlov put considerable effort into studying these examples of experimentally-induced neurosis, correlating them with different types and temperaments of animal, trying to understand their basis, and finding how best they might be relieved. The treatment of mental illness in the USSR today owes much to Pavlov's ideas and experiments on the subject.

In the West there is development of behaviour therapy using instrumental learning, in which situations to encourage people out of various phobic states, unacceptable sexual practices and suchlike are designed to produce forgetting of the old behaviour, and learning of new. The influence of the reinforcement principle spreads even further; its proponents are apt to regard almost anything from a kind word to a prison sentence as a reinforcement (positive or negative). Carefully considered and meted out, such reinforcements are used to try and control behaviour. Thus the Skinnerian version of the teaching machine

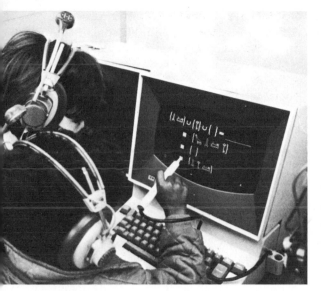

*A use of the reinforcement idea in the teaching machine. The smiling face indicates a correct response and constitutes a positive reinforcement. Negative reinforcement is a sad face complete with tear*

sustains high interest and rapid learning by means of a plentiful supply of positive reinforcements consisting of telling the student he has answered the question correctly (this can be achieved without deceit by writing the teaching programme in small, easily assimilated steps). Bonus and piece-rate schemes in industry may be thought of as following the same rules.

It has even been suggested that both Russian and American public attitudes have been moulded by their respective approaches to learning. More than one political commentator has remarked that the strategy of Soviet foreign policy seems to be to set up international Pavlovian conditioning situations with a view to inducing experimental neuroses in the minds of Western politicians. On the American side, foreign intervention is apparently seen by behavioural scientists, and (presumably) some US government technical advisers, as the problem of producing and sustaining so-called democratic behaviour in populations by the correct scheduling of the many different types of reinforcement available ranging from financial aid to burning villages and dropping bombs.

## Specific learning mechanisms

Although behavioural control in some circumstances is possible, the simple principles of classical or instrumental conditioning do not extend nearly as widely as is sometimes claimed. Learning is not to be understood merely as the formation of new connections in the brain between stimulus and response, nor is it the means by which any conceivable behaviour can be acquired, but the expression of rather specific mechanisms such as those for acquiring information about the availability of food in the environment, or for avoiding certain unpleasant events. Though it is, for instance, very easy to train a pigeon to peck at a small round disc to obtain access to food, it is difficult or impossible to train it to peck a disc to avoid electric shock. On the other hand, pigeons will learn relatively easily the response of running to the other end of a box in order to avoid shock. Apparently running is innately more appropriate to avoiding than is pecking, and is therefore more easily learned in these circumstances.

Even more striking is the finding that special kinds of learning exist, appropriate to specific situations. For learning about the things in the outside world it is important for events which are causally connected to be associated by the brain, and in general causality is reflected by events occurring one immediately after another. We operate a switch, and immediately the light goes on. It is just such sequences that are easily learned, but if the interval between one event and another is made longer than a few seconds, learning becomes difficult or impossible. Seemingly the learning mechanism reflects the temporal constraints of the majority of causal sequences.

In becoming ill, however, causality has a much longer time course, and something we ate may not take effect for several hours. The normal mechanism for learning about the outside world would be incapable of dealing with this time lag, but a special type of learning has been discovered with quite different characteristics. The mechanism associates the tastes and

*Rats can select a healthy diet, and apparently do so partly by means of a special learning mechanism that allows them to avoid tastes and smells which are followed several hours later by feelings of illness*

smells of the food that has been eaten with the feelings of becoming ill, or recovering from (for example) a vitamin deficiency. It is because of this mechanism that special poisons that do not produce a feeling of illness are needed to kill wild rats, and it is presumably also for this reason that after a stomach upset we find it difficult to face whatever we last ate.

A wealth of important knowledge has been acquired by using behavioural techniques to measure abilities of animals, but these advances should not necessarily be taken as signifying the truth of some of the rather rigid attitudes held by some neo-behaviourists such as Skinner, who largely ignore everything but reinforcement effects and eschew theory or explanation, setting out instead to find the best way to control behaviour. In a memorable phrase expressing both an apt comparison with Sherrington's surgically produced puppet-animals and this lack of concern with explanations, the Skinner box has been described as the best means so far invented for simultaneously decerebrating both the subject and the experimenter.

In order to understand the mechanisms of learning, or to reap benefits from social applications, it seems sensible not to be carried away, either by assertions that all higher mental activity is founded upon the conditioned reflex, or by the idea that any behaviour can be produced and manipulated using the reinforcement principle. There is much that we do not yet grasp about the nature of learning, but what we do know indicates that neither of these views offers a complete account of behaviour.

## Resistance to damage

Some decisive steps in the search for understanding learning were taken by Karl Lashley, who did much to dispel early assumptions about it being simply a matter of the formation of connections between stimulus and response. Lashley trained rats in different kinds of maze. Before training, some animals had various pieces of cortex removed in varying amounts until in a series of rats, each part of the cortex had been removed in some of the animals, and until the amounts of total cortex removed ranged up to 50 per cent or more. The learning of these rats was then compared with that of control animals which had received similar training but had their cortex intact. In another series of experiments rats first learned a maze, and then parts of the cortex were removed. Their retention of learning was compared with intact control animals.

Following the cortical removal, rats were still able to perform, though not quite so well. Lashley concluded that no specific part of the cortex was necessary for learning a maze, but that the rather unexpectedly small deterioration in learning was dependent simply on the amount of cortex that had been removed. Furthermore, although cortical removal after the learning had taken place, produced some deterioration in the rat's memory of the maze, again no specific part of the cortex seemed to be involved.

Not surprisingly, Lashley's work described in 1929 was attacked vigorously. These results seemed to strike at the very foundations of every sensible idea of both innate and learned connections in the brain. How could an animal respond appropriately to maze stimuli with nerve pathways missing? How could learning conceivably take place if connections between one part of the brain and another were not formed? Why was it that remembered items of the

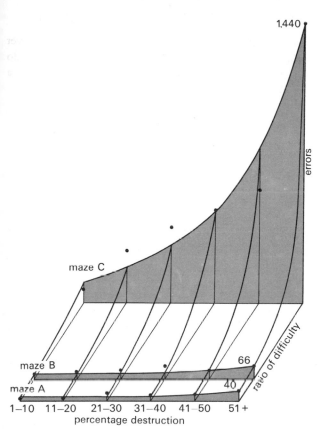

1,440

errors

maze C

maze B

maze A

66

40

ratio of difficulty

1–10  11–20  21–30  31–40  41–50  51 +

percentage destruction

*The relation between extent of cortical destruction and the number of errors in three progressively more difficult mazes used by Lashley. On the simpler mazes (A and B) quite severe damage had little effect on performance*

kind that must be involved in learning a maze were not localized in any particular place and totally destroyed by a lesion in one area or another?

Lashley redoubled his efforts, parried some of the methodological criticisms laid against him and in 1950, towards the end of a life of active experimentation and debate, wrote, 'I sometimes feel in reviewing the evidence on the localization of the memory trace, that the necessary conclusion is that learning just is not possible. It is difficult to conceive of a mechanism which can satisfy the conditions set for it.'

This last remark could not be more apt. What conceivable mechanism could continue to work with enormous parts of it destroyed? How is it that in our own brains perhaps as many as a hundred thousand neurones die every day, never to be replaced, and yet the whole brain continues to operate satisfactorily? Lashley's work marked an end to theories about stimuli being connected to responses in the way that two telephones are connected by wires through a series of exchanges. It is clear that some brain lesions do have specific effects on behaviour, for instance brain cancers in certain parts of the human cortex can cause loss of speech. But it is also clear that most cortical lesions cause far less disruption of the capacity to behave than might be expected from the amount of cortex destroyed. This conclusion demonstrates something of fundamental importance, namely that the brain has properties of overall reliability in the face of damage to its parts far in excess of any artificial machine that we yet have.

Lashley's own view was that the resistance to damage was somehow built into the organization of the brain, and that various parts were capable of taking over the functions of each other. There is nothing too strange about this notion. Factories carry on with only a mild drop in general efficiency when a 'flu epidemic temporarily removes 10 per cent of the staff, and armies notoriously continue fighting in the face of even larger depredations. People in most kinds of social organization can, and do, substitute for each other. In such organizations each unit (a person) is very complex and can take part in many different functions of the whole organization. At the same time, any particular function of the whole requires the participation of a large number of units.

The difficulty though was to conceive a physical mechanism that had these properties. Since Lashley's death a mathematical theorem has been proved showing that a computer could work despite damage to its parts if it had complex components arranged in the way just described for a social organization. Furthermore, an actual physical system, the hologram, has been invented that behaves rather as the brain was found to. Any part of a hologram can be removed, and the whole picture can still be reconstituted from small

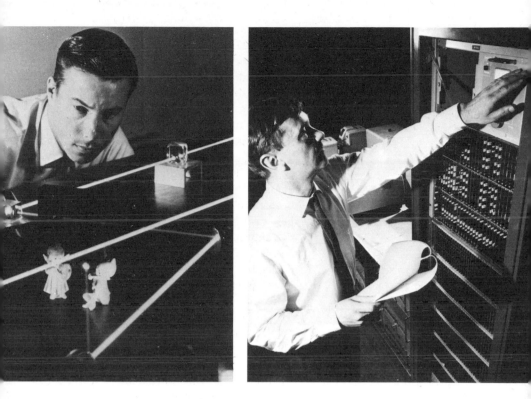

remaining pieces of the original hologram, though loss of definition occurs.

Computers which go on working even when some components fail would be an immense advance particularly for places where they cannot be serviced. At present a single component malfunction almost invariably causes nonsense in most computers since the whole rationale of computation depends upon every logical operation being exact and unfailing. Computers are being developed, however, which are resistant to damage and malfunction, though at present the means they employ, which might, for instance, involve performing all operations in triplicate and then taking a majority vote, are very simple.

Another possible type of explanation of the brain's extraordinary resistance to damage is that the effect depends not so much on the organization of neural

*Left: the hologram, a photographic record of the interference pattern between light direct from a laser and the laser light reflected from some object, has some of the properties of the cortex. If part of the hologram is removed the whole image can still be reconstituted. Right: this computer at the Standard Telecommunication Laboratories is a first step towards making computer hardware as reliable as brain tissue. It goes on working correctly despite any component malfunction, and when any circuit board is removed*

connections but on general principles underlying perception, learning and so forth. Everything we do depends upon being able to use rather fragmentary and disjointed patterns from the sense organs; for instance, we see a solid and stable visual world despite a disjointed succession of glances. Furthermore, we can recognize patterns whose parts are obscured or damaged. For ins   nce th  ugh there is  ome los  of eff ci ncy, it  s po s ble to rea   this se t nce   ith 20 p r cent of th  l t ers mis ing. We can also see quite well when looking through a mud-spattered window. Any mechanism that can cope in the ordinary way with these disruptions could also cope with damage of its own internal components. Indeed, for the most part the effect of damage to a few units in some parts of the mechanism might be exactly equivalent to blurring or obscuration of some part of the sensory pattern arriving from the outside world.

If the problem were not posed by the brain, but by a computer, it would boil down to the question of whether the resistance to damage was in the hardware or the program. As far as the brain goes, whichever conclusion is drawn from Lashley's work, something more subtle than telephone-wire connections between stimulus and response is required.

One result of Lashley's work has been redoubling of effort to specify what exactly an animal does learn. Do animals learn movements (responses) or do they learn about places, and the effects of actions? Do animals take in the whole of a stimulus situation, or do they concentrate on aspects of it?

Some of Lashley's own experiments stimulated the theory that when learning a problem rats entertain, as it were, hypotheses about what might be correct solutions. They first pay attention to one aspect of the stimulus situation, learning whether that aspect is regularly connected with reward. If not, they switch attention to another aspect, and so forth. This postulate, simple though it is, has extensive implications, many of which have been worked out in ingenious experiments by N. S. Sutherland and N. J. Mackintosh.

The attention idea which forms the basis of a good example of modern learning theory predicts and explains some surprising facts about learning. For instance, an animal can be trained to discriminate between two stimuli, being rewarded for (say) approaching vertical stripes, but not horizontal ones, and this training can be continued for some time after the animal has achieved correct performance. If now the reward is switched to be associated with the horizontal stripes, one might suppose that animals which had received a greater amount of training would take longer to reverse their behaviour. In fact they reverse performance more quickly, and this is what is predicted by the attention model. Attention is firmly attached to the horizontal-vertical aspect of the discrimination shapes, and not to other aspects of the stimuli, e.g. the size or the position of the stimuli which were not consistently associated with reward. Consequently the more highly trained animal maintaining its attention on the important aspect of the stimulus (horizontal – vertical) merely has to switch its responses to the member of the pair which was not previously rewarded.

This is not the only theory which today gives an account of the kinds of information processing that take place when an animal learns, and the subject is complex. What is clear from a large number of experiments, and from any of the theories that even begin to predict the behaviour that actually occurs, is that the stimulus-response notion which treats learning simply as the strengthening of connections between stimuli and responses under the influence of reinforcement, though it once looked promising was altogether too simple to explain the subtleties of behaviour.

## The physiological basis of memory

The ability of animals to learn has allowed physiological investigation of the change that takes place in the nervous system as a result of experience. Many people argue that the discovery of this change would open up a new era of investigation, much as the discovery of the genetic code has stimulated molecular biology.

From everything we know about brain mechanisms it seems most likely that information is stored by changing the transmission properties of systems of synapses. Thereby the properties of neural networks would be altered and the change could directly affect behaviour, although as Lashley showed, the pattern of new interconnections would be anything but simple. In recent years another possibility has been advanced. When delivered with the right sort of confident rhetoric, or when heard in a suitably receptive frame of mind, the argument can seem quite persuasive. It goes something like this: 'What is it that is so striking about memory? Why, that it lasts so long, and is so impervious to disruptions of brain activity that occur if we are banged on the head, or even when we go to sleep each night. No more permanent and indestructible form of storage can be imagined than a chemical, whose molecular structure is closely specified. Furthermore, it is information that needs to be stored, and one of the greatest advances in biology this century has shown that genetic information, the remembered inheritance of the species, is carried in a molecular structure. Why should not the experience of the individual then be stored in the same biochemical kind of way as the experience of the species?'

Biochemists have, therefore, made extracts of the brains of trained animals, and analysed them for changes in RNA. Even more ambitiously, some experimenters have administered such extracts to untrained animals to see if the recipients could perform the task that the donor animals had learned. For a while, the fact that scientists (perhaps unwisely) tend to publish only positive results, while consigning negative ones to the waste-paper basket, encouraged a few people to believe that the existence of 'memory molecules' had been established. It is now clear though that most of the positive experiments claiming identification, or transfer from one animal to another of a memory molecule, were speciously interpreted, or simply used the wrong types of learning task to carry conviction. For example, many of the experiments

*A model of a minute part of a ribonucleic acid molecule (RNA). This information-carrying molecule acts as an intermediary between genetic material and protein synthesis and has been considered as a candidate for information storage by learning, but the evidence is unconvincing*

were confused because the animals' task was merely to respond faster or slower, performance which is affected by motivation as well as learning. Instead, discrimination tasks, which require the animal to possess information, should have been used.

However, some biochemical changes certainly seem to occur specifically during learning, and there are also drugs, particularly those affecting protein synthesis, which affect learning and retention. It seems likely, however, that the fundamental changes underlying learning do take place at synapses, as the older idea had it, and there is electron microscope evidence for this. But since the change may involve growth, and growth requires protein synthesis, and protein synthesis depends upon RNA, the macromolecules have got into the act after all, though in a rather different role than before.

Though the possibility of information acquired during the life of the individual being stored in molecular structures as such now seems remote, there seems little doubt that methods by which information is stored in neural networks will be discovered in the next few years. It seems likely, moreover, that storage will be found to involve either growth, atrophy, or change in the metabolism of transmitter substances, at synapses.

However, it is not the process of storing information that constitutes the major problem for understanding. A piece of paper stores the words I am writing on it much better than my brain can. A slab of concrete stores information about where someone stepped in it before it set. Any lasting change brought about by the action of one process on another stores information, and there is no special difficulty about conceiving such storage in the brain. What is difficult to understand is the organization of stored information, and the means for its interpretation and subsequent employment. It is in such matters that human and animal memory is different from the unset concrete which can store but not put the stored information to use.

At two levels, therefore, the problems are not those

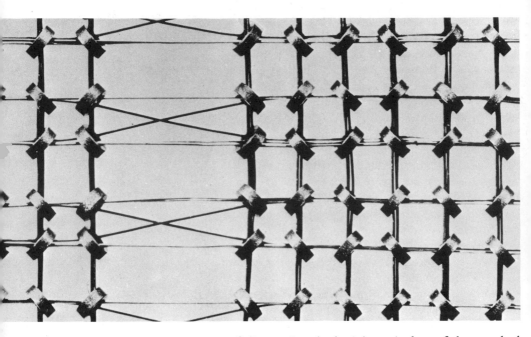

*Storing information as such is not a problem: a computer does it by magnetizing small ferrite rings by passing an electric current through them, 'reading' the stored information by passing another current in the opposite direction. What is difficult to understand is the organization of remembered information*

of discovering the brain's equivalent of the punched holes and magnetic changes which are the means by which a computer stores information. First, Lashley's results indicate that information in the brain is organized in such a way as to be resistant to local damage. Secondly, there is the question of what mechanisms select, organize, and retrieve information in the forms of learning which have been discovered in animals and men. These problems would be brought little if any nearer to solution if we did know what the underlying physiological mechanisms of storage were.

## Human memory

In a lifetime each of us probably stores thousands of millions of items although many of them are soon forgotten. There is evidence, for instance, that on reading an array of letters, we retain a sort of visual image of the array, which we can interrogate for up to a second afterwards.

Verbal material can be stored for a somewhat longer period in a store that retains the acoustic characteristics of a few items. In fact, most people can remember between five and nine items in this short-term memory store where an item is a word, a letter or a number. This sort of memory is especially good for holding telephone numbers while we dial them. But it too decays rapidly. Although its duration can be extended, continually re-filling the store by saying the words over and over again under our breath, this short-term memory is no good for long-term purposes. What it may be used for (and a possible reason why it arose before telephones were invented) is to hold strings of words temporarily while sentence structure is analysed. In the sentence you are reading now, for instance, the subject comes near the end. It may be that the mechanisms which analyse sentences have a preferred order of dealing with the different elements, e.g. subject first, main verb second and so forth. If any such constraints exist then the short-term verbal memory may bridge the gap between the order in which words arrive and the order in which sentences are analyzed.

The major problems of memory, though, are of the long term storage of knowledge. How is it that of all the things that we do know, a particular thing can be found and used at a moment's notice? It is possible for us to remember words which answer questions like 'What four-legged animal barks?' immediately and with no thought at all. Yet imagine how such an

*We usually use rather arbitrary indexing schemes to arrange any large quantity of information, such as in a library. Our own memories, however, have anything but an arbitrary organization, and somehow permit rapid access to stored information*

answer could be produced if all we had were lists of items arranged in alphabetical, or any other arbitrary order, or if we had to play a 'twenty questions' game in order to find them. Suppose we had forgotten the word 'dog', but had access to a large library filled with books, we might first locate a zoological treatise to find a list of four-legged animals describing the behaviour of each, or we might find a dictionary and look up 'bark', finding first that it meant the covering of a tree, secondly to scrape the skin of one's knuckles, thirdly a type of sailing ship, and at last the cry of a dog (which we might then have to make sure was a four-legged animal).

Clearly no scheme in which an arbitrary listing is consulted can begin to cope even with the simplest problems of human memory. For the same reason the idea that memory is like a cinema film of everything that has happened to us, and that we replay it when we remember something, must be totally mistaken. How do we identify which bit we want to replay? Do we run the film through until the part that we want occurs? The cinema film idea turns out to be hopeless as an explanation of memory. We memorize something by incorporating it into a complex pre-existing structure of knowledge which is largely self-consistent, and when we recall, we use large areas of this knowledge to reconstruct what must have happened.

An instructive way of introducing the problem of memory to a class of students is to arrange for someone to rush into the room at the beginning of a lecture and announce some emergency; for instance, 'A professor

Original Drawing

Reproduction 1

Reproduction 2

Reproduction 3

Reproduction

has just crashed his car into the computer room and it has caught fire. Can you dial 999 for the police and I will try and find the University rescue team?' The little drama need not last for more than a few seconds: and then the lecturer shamefacedly admits it was all a put-up job, but would everyone write down what they saw and heard.

Results of such unworthy pranks indicate that memory is quite unlike a cinema film, and many different versions will probably be produced. In some, 'A professor' may have acquired the name of the head of the department; in some the computer may have caught fire; in others it may be the car; others may write about summoning the fire brigade and so on. One wonders when people give evidence in court whether justice is ever done, particularly when months rather than minutes separate the event from its recall.

What seems to occur when we try to recall an event is that a few outstanding features of the scene are remembered (accurately or otherwise) and the rest of the series of events is fabricated around them. We remember what must have taken place or been said. Nor is such a memory any less vivid for being largely a reconstruction. In fact, the larger part of memory seems to be such reconstructions, and we can only fabricate such recollections within the terms of our model of the world, our structure of stored knowledge about what the world is like.

Though we still have a very inadequate understanding of these processes Frederic Bartlett, who was for many years Professor of Psychology at Cambridge,

*The results of one of Bartlett's experiments on memory: a slightly unusual, hieroglyphic owl becomes transformed during successive reproduction over a number of weeks into a familiar and conventional cat*

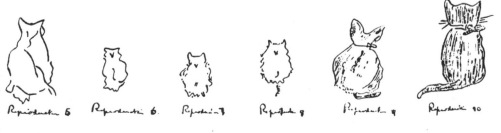

did much to point them out and started to describe the basic phenomena. His main experimental tool, suggested to him by Norbert Wiener, the founder of cybernetics, was a variation of the party game of 'rumour', in which an unlikely story passes from person to person and comes back in a rather different form. Bartlett used pictures and stories; but instead of having subjects recount them to each other, he had each subject reproduce the same material at intervals of a week or so, for periods up to a year or more.

With successive reproductions, changes took place: the stories or pictures were not stored in any fixed way but underwent a process of systematic and sometimes extensive reconstruction. A few individual highlights of the original material were found to be rather stable, and formed, as it were, the fixed points around which reconstruction took place. Significantly, the direction of change was generally in the direction of conventionalization. Exotic or unusual aspects of the original, or anything unfamiliar, become changed into more conventional accounts.

Bartlett used the term 'schemata' to describe the structures into which new information is incorporated, and which control the reconstructive process. They represent schematized knowledge and opinions which each individual has about what the world is like.

On the subject of reconstruction Ulric Neisser has proposed the appropriate metaphor of a paleontologist piecing together what a dinosaur must have been like from the evidence of a few chips of bone, and his knowledge of anatomy. A final form of the construction, perhaps a model of the flesh-covered dinosaur for a museum, need not even include the chips of bone.

The problems of memory thus cease to be 'How does storage of information take place?' but 1. 'How is knowledge of the world organized?' 2. 'How does the knowledge inform the reconstructive processes, and generate behaviour?' 3. 'How is new knowledge incorporated into mental schemata?' and 4. 'How do these structures themselves change with the passage of

time or the growth of understanding?' We have rather little idea about any of these questions, though for verbal information it is possible to guess what a schema embodying our knowledge of the world might be like, and how information can be stored in a way that is not arbitrary, but in some sense reflects the characteristics of what is stored.

For purely verbal information we might guess initially that schemata represent networks of associations between items that arise either from convention or from more fundamental inter-relationships in the world. Putting it in another way, one can suppose that words are stored in structures the interconnections of which signify the relationships that entities to which the words refer actually have. A simple case of such a structure would be a hierarchial arrangement which could be drawn as a tree diagram. A family tree is an example of this, in which people referred to at any one level are ancestors of those below, and progeny of

*Nobody has ever seen a Stegosaurus – rather like memory it is a reconstruction from extensive understanding, and fragmentary specific information*

those above. Lines here represent the relationship 'parent-child' and the sign = represents union (and often marriage). Other uses of the hierarchial arrangement might denote that items at the higher level actually contain those at a lower level, or lead to them or dominate them in some way.

Hierarchical organization is only one of the possible ways of inter-relating things, and any given item will take part in very many types of inter-relationships. As well as hierarchical relationships there is 'similar to' (e.g. paper-parchment), 'often accompanied by' (e.g. boy-girl), 'caused by' (e.g. sun-daylight) and many more. The extent of knowledge that is encompassed in a relationship structure must be both immense and detailed. The total of these kinds of inter-relations (which may be called semantic, and in some sense reflect the structure of the world), comes close to defining the meaning of any item. From such a structure we could give an exhaustive dictionary definition by reading off the types of relationships which an item had with others. Many items presumably would also be interconnected with stored knowledge about how they are perceived visually or by hearing, touch and so on.

Items might also take part in another totally separate set of purely verbal associations. A verbal relationship exists for instance between bookshop and bookmaker, even although the items themselves are semantically unrelated.

Various ways of investigating which words are inter-related have been used. One is simple free-association: 'Say the first word that comes into your head.' This technique gives exactly the type of conventional associations that one would expect; 'knife–fork', 'bus–stop', 'furcoat–expensive', and occasionally less conventional ones; 'coffin–spittin'. But the trouble is that though a list of associations may tell one which words are interconnected, it does not tell one what types of inter-relationship any given association represents. What one ends up with is something like Roget's *Thesaurus*; a collection of lists of interconnected words, but still lacking the essential structure that provides the basis for thought and reflects the nature of the world.

It seems likely, for instance, that thoughts are enabled to flow smoothly by moving through such structures of ordered inter-relationships (and further discussion of this appears towards the end of Chapter 10). The extent to which thought is original may depend upon the richness of interconnections, and the extent to which associations other than the conventional ones exist or can be produced. It is interesting that in ordinary speech the longest pauses between words occur not so much where the white spaces or punctuation marks occur in print (there are no real pauses between most spoken words, as may easily be ascertained by listening to someone speaking a foreign language), but before the unconventional or unusual word.

Finding how both verbal and non-verbal information is stored is one of the most challenging tasks of brain research. The means whereby it is achieved, if translated into computer programs, would have the most profound practical consequences. What is more, it seems likely that until we understand what knowledge is stored in the brain and how it is arranged, many other problems will also remain unsolved.

The emergence of language may well have been the most important factor in man's evolutionary success. It seems to provide much of the basis for logical thought, but perhaps even more significantly, language provides a channel, which by now must rival the capacity of the genetic apparatus, for transmitting information from generation to generation. Newton might have spoken for us all when he said 'If I have seen further, it is by standing on the shoulders of giants'. We owe most of our knowledge to the fact that discoveries need to be made just once by a remarkable man for them to become public property.

Man's capacity for language, unrivalled though it is in other animals, must presumably be founded upon capacities for dealing with the world that were present in our ancestors at a pre-human stage of evolution, and some of these capacities may be present in higher apes now. At least two recent experimental projects have claimed some success in teaching chimpanzees some element of human language.

## Verbal behaviour versus language

The behaviourists stressed the close relationships between the abilities of man and sub-human animals, claiming that differences were largely ones of degree. It was in this spirit that Skinner in 1957 published his book *Verbal Behaviour*. He argued that the principle of reinforcement, relevant to a rat pressing a lever and perhaps to a gambler operating a one-armed bandit, is

*Sarah the chimpanzee, it is claimed, has been taught some elements of language. Apes cannot make speech sounds but Sarah uses plastic tokens on a board as linguistic symbols*

just as relevant to learning and maintaining language. Undifferentiated sounds first made by an infant are shaped by parental reinforcement to produce words. Names said in the presence of the appropriate object also receive reinforcement, as do patterns of words, until eventually reinforcement principles ensure an ability to use the whole language.

To those who had become accustomed, and perhaps conditioned, to thinking of the Skinner box as a microcosm in which to study all behaviour, Skinner's account may have seemed acceptable, but to others it was not. Amongst these others was the linguist Noam Chomsky, who in the last few years has revolutionized the study of language. In one of the splendid clashes with which brain research seems to abound Chomsky has confronted neo-behaviourism. The debate started in Chomsky's long and detailed review of Skinner's book.

In *Verbal Behaviour*, Skinner claimed that a child acquires language because of the careful arrangement of reinforcing contingencies by the people around him. It is obvious that we do acquire the particular language that we are brought up with, and that we must acquire it by learning from what we hear. What seems more questionable, though, is that the adults all carefully arrange reinforcements to encourage correct grammatical speech in children. What, for instance, is there in common between the judicious use of food to teach a dog to beg, and the way a child learns to talk?

*Skinner's characterization of language learning invokes the picture of teaching an animal tricks. To Chomsky and many other linguists and psychologists the reinforcement analysis seems inappropriate*

Chomsky pointed out that some parents may conscientiously try to shape the child's language, but equally an immigrant child learns with surprising ease and accuracy from his playfellows a language his parents can scarcely speak.

Any stimulus–response theory is based on the notion that, either by way of innate connections or learned ones, a pattern of stimulation causally determines a pattern of response. In conformity with this principle, Skinner claims that responses can come 'under the control of extremely subtle properties of stimuli', so that on being shown a painting we might say 'Dutch'. We are apparently responding to the property Dutchness. By the same argument if we were to say 'Clashes with the wallpaper', we must presumably be responding to clashfulness-with-the-wallpaper. Clearly reinforcement theory not only makes a poor job of identifying the stimulus except by reference to what the response was, but it is also forced into the position of having to suppose that every pattern of words that we produce is caused by some distinctive stimulus pattern, that has in some way been associated with reinforcement.

## Chomsky's linguistics

Chomsky's work on language starts from a totally different standpoint. He argues that we have the ability to understand (and create) an infinite number of sentences. It is unlikely, for instance, that you have previously come across the sentence that you are reading now, but unless I make a mistake of some sort it should be possible for you to understand it. The fact that language is essentially creative so that we can understand and produce totally new sentences, is outside the range of a system of simple learned responses to stimuli. Such a system would be capable of dealing only with increasing the probability of behaviours that have happened before.

It is also instructive that neither in children nor in adults is there much (if any) trial and error language, that might be described as 'I wonder if this set of sounds will make the sentence that means what I want to say?' Many mistakes are made in ordinary speech – not because we have to learn how to use each new sentence, but because of such things as our memory being too limited for the particular sentence construction that we are using, so that we forget what we are saying. On the other hand we do not make many purely grammatical mistakes. Chomsky illustrates this idea of 'grammatical' by two sentences:

1. *Colourless green ideas sleep furiously.*
2. *Furiously sleep ideas green colourless.*

In ordinary speech we would not produce either of these sentences. It is also clear that whereas both are nonsense, the second is ungrammatical nonsense. Chomsky therefore argues both that it is possible to separate grammar from meaning, and that since we can produce indefinitely many grammatical sentences without producing ungrammatical ones we must know the grammar of English. This knowledge he calls grammatical competence, and it may be regarded as a set of rules by which all the grammatical sentences of a language could be formed (even though there is an infinite number of such sentences) but without forming any ungrammatical strings of words.

Clearly competence does not imply that any English speaker could give explicit answers to questions such as 'Can you decline the present tense of the verb 'to be'?', or 'What is a gerund?'. Most people could not. But the fact that they use these parts of speech correctly, indicates just as surely that they know the grammar. The knowledge, in other words, is largely unconscious, but it is nevertheless fundamental.

The idea of competence, what we must in some sense know to be able to act in some way, can be separated from the idea of performance which involves questions of how in particular the knowledge is represented in the brain and what mechanisms produce behaviour on the basis of it. In order not to prejudge how performance depends upon competence, when giving an account of this underlying knowledge we have to be careful to express it in the most neutral way possible. The importance of competence is that it is primary. It would be difficult or impossible to understand performance correctly if our idea of the underlying competence were basically wrong.

The way in which linguists expose competence despite its largely unconscious nature, is to make up sentences of various kinds, and appeal to readers to agree with them that the sentences are either acceptable or unacceptable (i.e. anomalous). Or they might ask whether two different sentences have a similar interpretation (paraphrase), or whether a single sentence has more than one interpretation (ambiguity). By following this technique, together of course with a good deal of intuition about what sentences to choose, linguists have begun to work out a grammar for English. On the one hand a sentence is a sequence of sounds which we might hear or utter. On the other hand, the sentence has a meaning. The grammar is a system of rules that relates the sounds to the meaning, and unravelling it is therefore essential for any understanding of language.

Chomsky claims that sentences have what he calls a deep structure, hidden beneath the order of the words, but related to the meaning of the sentence. He uses the demonstrations of ambiguity and paraphrase to reveal this underlying structure. Consider the sentence.

*Flying planes can be dangerous.*

This single order of words can have either of two meanings which may be loosely paraphrased as follows: (a) 'Piloting planes can be a dangerous occupation', and (b) 'Planes flying around can be dangerous to people nearby'. Beneath the order of the words lie two different possible grammatical structures one of which carries the implication of someone flying planes, while the other uses 'flying' as a qualifying term equivalent to planes 'which fly'.

Chomsky's contribution to the elucidation of the nature of the grammar that relates deep structure to the strings of words that form sentences was that he proposed entirely objective and explicit sets of rules whereby some types of grammatical sentences could be generated without generating ungrammatical strings of words. These rules can be applied in an absolutely mechanical way, without it being necessary to exercise judgement about what to do to form a grammatical sentence. Instead the rules themselves display what kind of judgement (or knowledge) is exercised by a person in being able, for instance, to see which word is the subject of some sentence. Chomsky has proposed two sets of such rules, one set for forming basic sentences which have deep structure, and another set of transformational rules operating upon deep structures to generate what he calls surface structures which underlie the sentences we speak or hear.

A single deep structure is rather like a set of relationships connecting the elements of a single idea. Putting it another way, certain elements and their relationships might represent something we know, like 'John has gone to the library'. But in their deep structure these elements and relationships are what one might call a raw form and denote only that 'John' is related to 'library' by the past tense of the verb 'to go'. (See the last part of Chapter 10 for some discussion of the way in which such relationship structures might be stored in memory.) The point is that although the deep structure can be interpreted to indicate the relationship between 'John' and 'library', this structure has to be transformed to produce a surface structure which underlies the form of words we would actually use when saying something about this matter.

It may be that, for some very simple sentences such as 'The man hit the ball', deep and surface structures would be rather similar, and indeed Chomsky uses this sentence to illustrate the way in which the first set of basic rules operates to generate a deep structure, and the words that relate to it. In general though both the basic set, and the transformational set of rules have to be applied to generate a sentence corresponding to the form of words that we would actually speak. Indeed,

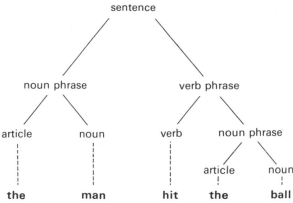

*The internal structure of a sentence is illustrated by this hierarchical diagram. The grammatical structure is shown joined by dotted lines to the 'terminal string' — words in the sentence which can be slotted into place as 'noun', 'verb', and so on*

Chomsky has described the difference between his and other theories of grammar by saying that whereas they suppose that deep and surface structure are identical, the central idea of his transformational grammar is that these structures are different. A syntactic process transforms deep into the surface structure (and *vice versa*) by the repeated application of certain rules. Quite distinct from this are the two interpretive processes, one of which relates surface structures to sound patterns, and another, semantic one, which relates deep structure to meaning.

It is not even the case that words relate in a simple one-to-one fashion with patterns of sound. For instance, the same sound pattern can be used for

*A speech spectrogram of a man saying 'Santa Claus'. The calibration mark on the left shows frequency bands of 500 cycles per second. This type of visible record of the intensities and frequencies of speech over time allows us to see that very different physical patterns can still be understood as the same word*

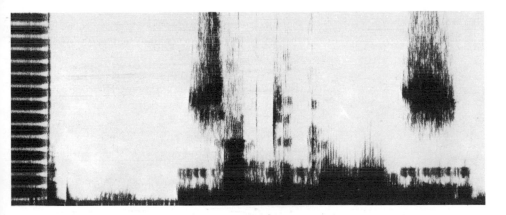

different words (e.g. to, too, two) and the same word can be heard in different physical sounds (e.g. as made by male and female voices). It seems certain, therefore, both from grammatical and phonological considerations, that very complex structures and processes do underlie language.

As one final example of the importance of structure beneath the order of words, consider the sentence:

*Mary is happy.*

We all know (i.e. our linguistic competence includes rules for) how to form the question that relates to this declarative sentence. We reverse the order of 'Mary' and 'is'. Yet we cannot form a question simply by reversing the order of the first two words in any declarative sentence. Doing this to the sentence 'Mary's friend is happy', for instance, will not work. Transformations applied to produce a question, and indeed other kinds of linguistic transformation, apply not to the form and order of words but to structure within the sentence; to the organization of words into phrases such as 'Mary's friend'.

It is with this kind of demonstration that Chomsky and other linguists set out to discover what grammatical competence in English might consist of, although Chomsky is careful to stress that he is discussing not what a speaker or listener actually does. The transformational and other rules are not anything that a speaker or hearer might use to produce or understand sentences, they are merely a convenient way to characterize what he must in some sense know in order to do these things.

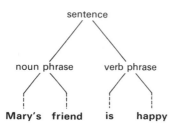

*The structure of this sentence shows that 'Mary's friend' is the noun phrase, which during transformation must be manipulated as a whole*

Nevertheless the implication is clear. In the same way that visual perception involves interpreting patterns of light as objects, toward which we could direct action, understanding a sentence involves recovering its meaning. This seems only to be possible via a very complex series of operations. It is not enough to say that if we were to remark, 'The weather does not look too good today', that this involves the activation by a pattern of light on the retina of a particular pattern of muscular movements of the vocal apparatus. Such an account either slides over the whole problem without saying anything at all about it, or else contains the misconception that behaviour relates to stimuli without the intermediary of meaning.

The basis of linguistic competence of even one language has barely begun to be worked out however, and the task is difficult, painstaking and highly technical. Though this work is central to linguistics the implications for the study of brain and mind may be even more far-reaching.

## Universal grammars

Each of us, native speakers of a language, acquires by the age of five or so, an extensive knowledge of a grammar, in the sense that we produce grammatical sentences but not sentences of the form:

*Friend Mary's is happy?*

This might mean that each child regardless of intelligence, starting without any preconceptions, hears sounds (which are not even related in a one to one fashion with words), and constructs a theory of the use of grammar within his mind. Each English or American child might work out entirely for himself on the basis of the very small sample of utterances that he hears, a complete grammar of English. Linguists, on the other hand, working for hundreds of years on the problem have been unable to work out explicitly more than a small fraction of the structure of this grammar.

There is a sense in which each child does work out the grammar, inducing general rules from small numbers of specific instances. But it seems clear that to be able to do this he must inherit very strong biases as to what kinds of inductions to make. He must possess foundations of a very specific kind, waiting, as it were, to receive any particular language, English, Chinese or whatever. On the basis of what might therefore be called a universal grammar which we all inherit, the specific grammar of our native language can be built. This universal grammar must be very restrictive, to allow the child to interpret the sounds he hears, and assign them roles in the specific structure of his language. Such restrictions as the permissible ways of forming a question, for instance, seem to be based on some innate bias for organizing groups of words into phrases. In no language are any transformations applied to the order of words as such, to form questions, negatives or passives. Reversing the order of the first two words, or ordering the words of a sentence in reverse, though they are examples of simple transformations upon word order, do not occur as grammatical rules and it is doubtful whether a grammar based on such transformations could ever be learned.

When a child learns to speak, he seems to exhibit some notions of grammar right from the time he puts two words together. The following sentences for instance, recorded by the psycholinguist Roger Brown, were among the first that a child called Adam ever produced:

> *Two boot.*
> *Hear tractor.*
> *A gas.*

Apparently to start with Adam used only three grammatical categories, noun, verb and modifier (e.g. two, a). Though in eight hours of recorded speech he produced 400 two-word sentences, he produced no ungrammatical orders such as 'boot two' or 'A hear'. Evidently Adam seemed from the first to be operating with structured sentences, rather than emitting word-pairs in a trial and error fashion. Furthermore, his sentences were so different from those uttered by adults around him as to make it very unlikely that the process can simply be passed off as a parrot-like imitation. He seemed to have made the generalization that the word-relationship 'followed by' could be applied in some circumstances but not in others.

## Children's concepts

What the individual learns seems to be dependent upon what innate structures can assimilate, i.e., a highly restrictive set of interpretations of sensory patterns. If auditory and visual data had to be learned about in all their possible arrangements, it seems unlikely that any individual within his lifetime would acquire a self-consistent set of mental operations to underlie perception, language and thought. Earlier chapters have been concerned with the way in which the brain contains structures capable of modelling, and thus capturing the significance of, things that happen in the world, and these mechanisms might be the same as, or similar to, what linguists call the universal grammar. One way to go about discovering what innate mental structures might be like, therefore, is to study the thoughts and concepts of young children. It is at the point of universal and unlearned modes of conceptualization that the work of the Swiss psychologist Jean Piaget meets this problem.

Piaget has found that babies at first seem not to have the notion of the permanence of an object. When out of sight an object effectively ceases to exist. At perhaps the age of nine months, however, they begin to search for an object if it disappears under or behind something else. Their mind begins to reflect the fact that in the real world objects have a permanent existence. Piaget has shown by a series of ingenious demonstrations how, later on, children begin to grasp concepts such as number, the volume of fluid and so forth.

The idea of conservation of a volume of water when

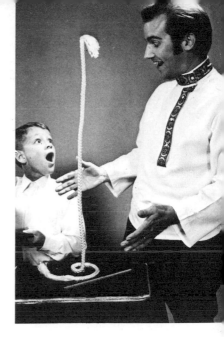

*Magic is surprising because it seems to contradict what we know about the mechanics of the world – perhaps children are particularly fascinated by it because they have not quite abandoned semi-magical explanations of natural phenomena, though the concept of permanence of objects which forbids sudden appearance and disappearance is grasped before 1 year of age*

*By the age of 6 or 7 most children know that the quantity of fluid does not change when poured from one vessel to another, despite different perceived heights of the liquid if the vessels are of different shapes, but they do not need to undertake a series of experiments to reach this concept empirically, nor is it clear what experience they could acquire which would allow them to reach this conclusion*

171

poured from a glass of one shape into a glass of another shape, and the abstract notion of number are not simple concepts however, and it is by no means clear that a child grasps them as conclusions derived from experiments with actual objects in the world. Reinforcement, or any other learning principle seems inadequate to explain how these notions of the nature of the physical world are acquired. It would be possible to regard each child as his own experimenter, coming at last to grasp the appropriate theoretical concept, but as for the acquisition of grammatical competence this seems unlikely. Furthermore, if the child did grasp such concepts on the basis of his own experiments, we would then have to ask why conservation of volume is grasped by nearly all children by the age of 8, whereas the idea of conservation of inertia is not.

Aristotle taught, and it was almost universally regarded as self-evident, that objects were either at rest, or naturally fell downwards. For an object to move in any other direction must therefore entail a force acting continuously upon it. The theory was self evident despite the fact that this gave all sorts of trouble with explaining what the forces were that kept arrows flying in their path, or marbles rolling on a flat surface. The modern idea of conservation of inertia, that every object remains at rest or travels uniformly in a straight line *unless* acted upon by a force, is now familiar to schoolchildren as Newton's first law of motion. This concept was not acquired until some of the world's greatest scientists and philosophers had observed, experimented, muddled and argued about it for two thousand years. Historians of science indeed tend to regard its enunciation as the leap which crossed man's greatest intellectual hurdle. Typical is Butterfield who describes this single step as 'the one most amazing in character, and the most stupendous in the scope of its consequences'. Only by virtue of our education (apparently) do we now recognize that a ball rolls unaided in a straight line across a billiard table.

One can only assume that in one case mental structures capable of receiving and interpreting the per-

*We are now quite happy with the idea of conservation of inertia, which holds that billiard balls roll until stopped by friction in straight lines (unless spin is applied) and predicts the angles and velocities of each ball after an impact. Before Newton, apparently innately reasonable views could not explain 'billiard-ball mechanics'*

ceived height of water in glasses of different shapes as being consistent with conservation of volume are innate, whereas mental structures interpreting motions of objects as continuing in a straight line unless acted upon by a force are not. In the first case it is not easy to see what programme of experimentation and hypothesis testing each child carries out or by what conclusions he is reinforced, or in the second why phenomena which received perhaps more observation and thought than any other in history can have been so refractory to a self-consistent formulation.

## Mechanisms of thought

Logical thought, as distinct from grammatical correctness, may well depend upon the same innate mechanisms which Chomsky has called the universal grammar. But to expose this fundamental logical competence in adults it may again be necessary to move away from study of language, just as Piaget has done for children. If we put together Craik's idea of mental processes modelling or symbolically representing reality, with Chomsky's idea of competence, then a means for finding out about some fundamental mental operations begins to suggest itself.

We can ask what a model of the world would need to represent. We can actually inspect the way in which things seem to us to occur in the world. If we then express our understanding (knowledge) of some particular set of events and their inter-relationships in the most general but at the same time most rigorous possible way, then we will have a competence model: a statement of what the brain must know about these objects and events. We can then inquire how far this particular piece of competence correctly expresses what the brain's model must contain to perform some piece of behaviour. In a more specific context, consider the concept of causality. Nothing could be more fundamental to logical thinking, or to the way in which we act and perceive events.

Expressing the matter in the most neutral and general terms, given two events $a$ and $b$ we might assign causal properties to sequences of $a$ and $b$ events where the probability of $b$ following $a$ was higher than chance. In other words, if the probability of $b$ happening alone were 10 per cent and the probability of $b$ occurring given that $a$ had happened were 90 per cent, this would be initial (but not conclusive) evidence for some kind of causal relationship between $b$ and $a$. We might therefore propose an initial hypothesis that if an observer judges that events are causally connected, he has the means for calculating the probability of $b$ given that $a$ has occurred and comparing the result with the probability of $b$ occurring independently of $a$. It is possible to express such a competence model even more formally in mathematical terms. It is also easy to imagine a machine, e.g. a computer, performing such a calculation. As set out above the notion of causality is expressed in a general way, so as to include both the obvious case in which $b$ never happens unless $a$ does, and the cases in which causality is no less present but may be obscured because of intermediate steps which can also be affected by various extraneous factors.

In a series of experiments by H. M. Jenkins and W. C. Ward, it was shown that even in situations where *b* does not invariably follow *a*, people are very eager to make statements and behave in a way that indicates that they perceive or judge *a* and *b* events to be causally connected. In one of Jenkins and Ward's experiments subjects were asked to find out how to press a set of buttons in such a way as to control the onset of two lights. Other subjects were also asked to witness the performance and judge how far the active subjects did succeed in causing the lights to switch on. Exactly the kind of underhand trick that many people suspect is employed in psychological experiments was played in this one. The experimenters arranged that the subjects' button-pushing had no effect whatever on the onset of the lights, and the experiment was run under various conditions, which differed only in the frequency with which lights came on. Subjects judged and behaved in such a way as to indicate that they understood particular patterns of button pushing (event *a*) to cause the lights to come on (event *b*), and they made this type of judgement so long as the lights came on reasonably often. But their judgements were quite independent of the conditional probability of *b* occurring given that *a* had.

Jenkins and Ward thus found that the competence model their subjects were using does not correspond to a general grasp of causal relationships in the world. People attribute significance to preceding (type *a*) events purely on the basis of whether following, or type *b*, events occur frequently. The brain apparently has no innate mental apparatus which will calculate whether the probability that *b* occurs given that *a* has just happened (the condition where causation could have been responsible) is any higher than the probability of *b* occurring whether or not *a* did.

Jenkins and Ward started off with the hypothesis that we might have an adequate competence for dealing with causality. But a simple and appropriate mathematical statement of wide generality did not

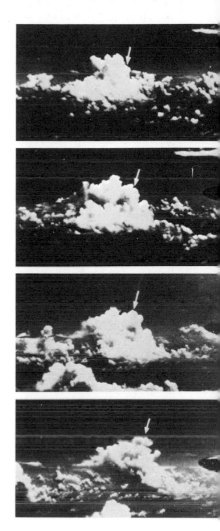

*A series of pictures showing attempts at seeding clouds to produce rain. As in Jenkins' and Ward's experiments, people given all the information about the results of such attempts usually judge them to have been successful if rain falls. They do not attribute success only when the probability of rain following seeding exceeds that following no seeding*

*Superstitions may be a result of our inability to perceive causality correctly. They develop particularly in times of stress, as with these wartime pilots. Over any range of experience the desired outcome (returning alive) has always occurred as far as a particular individual is concerned, and this high probability allows causal significance to become attached to irrelevant objects such as mascots*

actually correspond with the way the problem is treated by the brain. The brain chooses a simplicity of a different kind, neglecting to calculate conditional probability, and assigning causal significance simply on the basis of the likelihood with which the event of interest occurs at all. This simplification is perfectly adequate for many dealings with the world in which *b* events never happen at all unless an *a* event has just occurred. For example, doors do not open by themselves. As soon as this simple situation is not fulfilled, however, as soon as the caused event does not follow invariably and within a second or so of an immediately obvious causal event (the condition in which instrumental learning can occur), we are lost, and our brains fail to assimilate the situation.

For evidence of this one merely has to look at the history of medicine, where doctors have been able to thrive upon this universal mental defect. The fact that getting better from an illness is an event of high probability (as compared to dying) has allowed the medical profession to delude themselves and their patients down the ages that getting better was the result of a cure that they had administered. The letting of blood as a remedy for all types of illness, for instance, flourished for nearly two thousand years. At the height of this fashion Francois Broussais, who had been a surgeon in Napoleon's army, held – amongst other influential medical opinions – that most of the troubles of humanity were caused by stomach upsets, that the healing power of nature did not exist, and that starvation and the application of leeches for blood-letting would cure all diseases. His influence apparently so stimulated the leech industry that in the single year of 1833 forty million leeches were imported into France.

Scientific method, and in particular such activities as careful and repeatable experimentation, and more lately statistical analysis of data are, of course, precisely the means for compensating for our innate inability properly to perceive or appreciate causal relationships other than of the simplest kind. In so far as science has been successful, we have managed to circumvent this inbred inadequacy. On the other hand, if concepts such as the conservation of momentum do not leap immediately to mind, science may take an unconscionable time arriving at them.

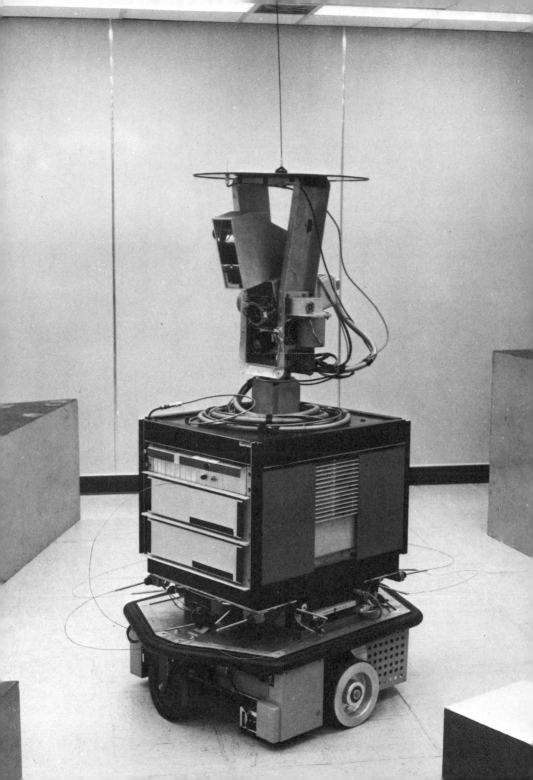

# ARTIFICIAL BRAINS 10

One of the most important points in any piece of brain research comes when the question is asked 'Can we make a working model that will produce the behaviour in question, and at the same time display basic principles that make the behaviour possible?' To program a computer to carry out operations which we have discovered in the brain is an inescapable test of understanding. The membrane theory of nerve impulses, the mechanism of thirst, the attention model of discrimination learning, and other problems have been simulated using computers. For any hypothesis with more than a few logical steps, or for any system in which variables change with time, such simulations are essential, since unaided the human mind is too frail to encompass all the processes at once, or (sometimes) to make sufficiently rigorous postulates, or to derive necessary conclusions.

There are many people who resent the invention of computers and fail to recognize them as the most important step in man's intellectual advance certainly since the introduction of writing, and perhaps since the beginning of language. Among their favourite gibes is that computers are used in science as a substitute for understanding. Although some scientists do waste time analysing data that they do not understand with computers whose programs they could not write, in the matter of simulation the gibe is wide of the mark. In order to write a program one must be able to instruct the computer step by painstaking step. No woolly

*Opposite: the Stanford Research Institute robot, an example of a complete mechanical behaving organism. Moving in an environment of blocks, it has a television camera eye, various other sensors, and a radio link to its brain (a rather large computer), but its behaviour is still limited because of immense gaps in our understanding*

thinking is allowed, no conclusions that do not follow strictly from the premises will be produced. A simulation, in other words, is the real test of exactly how much about some brain function we do understand. A computer exposes much more rigorously than we can the consequences of any hypothesis, and will demonstrate exactly how far the behaviour that occurs does follow from the understandings that we express in its program.

## Intelligent machines

For some problems it is not necessary to wait until we gain a thorough understanding of how the brain works. We can try to program computers immediately to play chess, prove mathematical theorems, or read handwriting. Here the task is to be able to invent a way in which these things could conceivably be done. In other words, we can try to see whether it is possible to establish aspects of mind in a device other than the human brain. Indeed, understanding how the biological brain performs functions of this kind may be heavily dependent upon ideas which have been sifted through the mill of invention of artificial brains that can perform them.

Understanding often seems to depend upon being able to see the correspondence between at least two disparate examples of the same property. In biology it often depends upon the comprehension of physical systems. We understand the electrical nature of nervous transmission by seeing correspondences between aspects of nerve cells and electrical processes familiar in physics and engineering.

The computer therefore provides two new and indispensable potentialities: first, it is the only physical device so far that has the intricacy of structure needed to represent adequately operations that are performed by the brain, and secondly it provides facilities for creating entirely new understandings of what it means to think, to speak or to see, with which we can compare the brain.

Rather than describing here any of the better-known

pieces of intelligent computer behaviour, I will return now to the problem of visual perception. It should then be possible to place the new insights obtained from actually trying to make a machine that will 'see' simple patterns in a meaningful way alongside the knowledge obtained from neurophysiology, psychology and the history of painting. By combining these forms of insight we may within the next few years be in a position to formulate with some rigour the kinds of mechanisms which underlie human perception.

## Essentials of seeing

The first thing trying to program a computer does is to concentrate the mind on essentials. In performing biological experiments it is easy to get diverted from the main objective into rather specific investigations of side issues. What then are the essentials of seeing? Three important points are as follows:

1. When we see, we can not only classify objects, but can describe their visual properties, and the relations of parts of a scene to each other. We do not just attach labels to particular retinal patterns in a stimulus–response sort of fashion.

2. The retina is a two-dimensional surface but we nevertheless see solid objects in a world of three dimensions. Evidently we must interpret the succession of two-dimensional patterns on the retina as arising from two-dimensional objects in space.

3. Any interpretive process capable of carrying out 1 and 2 presupposes knowledge of some properties of three-dimensional space, and the two-dimensional patterns it can give rise to. (The concept of this knowledge is equivalent to what Chomsky means by competence.)

Taking point 1, for instance, we would not be inclined to say that a machine could recognize human faces if we made outline figures of faces by bending pieces of wire, and constructed a machine containing templates which matched each of these outlines, with each template arranged to operate an illuminated panel

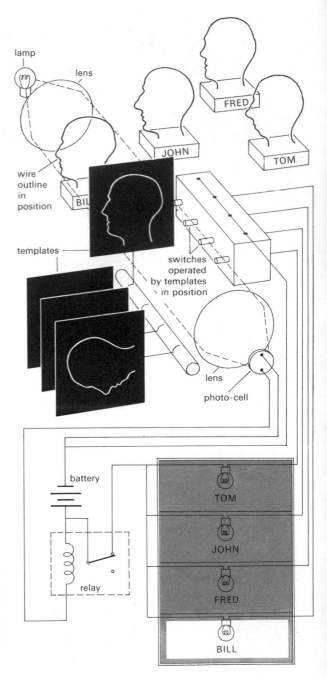

lamp

lens

wire
outline
in
position

templates

switches
operated
by templates
in position

lens

photo-cell

FRED

JOHN

TOM

BILL

battery

relay

TOM

JOHN

FRED

BILL

*This device will identify wire out-*
*lines of faces by comparing them*
*successively with templates, and*
*illuminating a name panel if a match*
*occurs. This is a stimulus-response*
*machine and we would be loth to say*
*that it could see*

displaying the name of the person whose face was depicted. It is easy to make such a device, by shining a light past each outline in turn, and onto a photo-cell. Only the template which exactly matched the outline would not admit any light to the photo-cell, which would then signal to a simple electrical circuit so that the name corresponding to the appropriate template was displayed.

This process, which corresponds closely to a stimulus–response formulation of seeing would be a caricature of what we normally understand by the term 'to see'. It is easy in this example to observe exactly the limitations of the notion that the brain acts as a network to interconnect stimulus and response. Nevertheless, based upon this principle, machines have been built to behave in a manner that could be mistaken for that of living animals. Nervous systems of this kind could work, and could deal with the physical world. It may be that insects are at least partly stimulus–

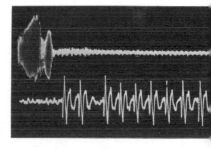

*Above: the echo-locating squeaks of a bat (top oscilloscope trace) are recognized by a moth, whose neural responses to that specific sound are displayed in the lower trace. On receiving the stimulus the moth seems to behave in a rather stimulus-response fashion, taking avoiding action by zig-zagging or dropping to the ground. In the time lapse photograph (left) this action is unsuccessful and at ( f ) the moth is finally caught by the bat*

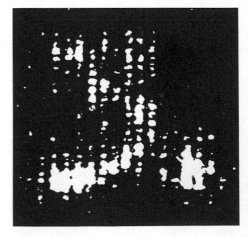

*Magnetic numerals on cheques are read by a template-matching device – but notice that a special standard type face has to be used*

*The type and handwritten characters that we can easily read are very varied (left) and often of poor quality (right). It is this kind of fact that template matching and most other mechanical pattern-recognition schemes founder upon. There is still no satisfactory way of reading hand-writing mechanically*

response organisms, responding with a finite set of motor patterns to a finite set of stimulus patterns.

Template-matching machines have been developed and refined, and within the context of a finite set of stimuli and responses they also work. Machines that read magnetic numerals on cheques are of this general type, though it is significant that a special set of numerals has been designed to suit the machine. Machines with added sophistication are being developed that will even allow classification of ordinary printed letters and numerals, despite poorness in the quality of print, variations of its size, position and orientation, and differences of the type face. Each of these problems can be attacked by transforming the input pattern in various ways to reach a standard form

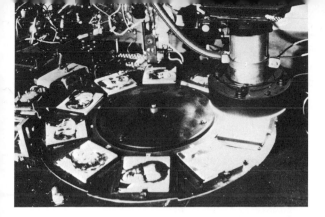

*UCLM II is a picture-classifying machine that learns – but this ability does not eliminate the serious deficiency of all stimulus–response machines, that they operate only within the framework of a limited set of input patterns and a limited set of responses*

or by storing many versions of the same letter. Machines of this class have even been constructed so that they learn to attach particular classifications to particular patterns. In other words, stimulus–response machines are capable of being made quite sophisticated and can cope to some extent with classifying the patterns they are designed for.

Their limitation is none the less real and profound. It is in fact just the same as that which Chomsky has pointed out in the stimulus–response analysis of language. Neither in language nor in perception are the necessary operations those of connecting superficial patterns of stimuli to superficial patterns of response. A concept like that of deep structure is needed, interpretable in language into the domain of meaning, and in perception into the domain of objects.

In perception the problem is not simply that of attaching the label 'chair' or whatever to particular patterns. We recognize a chair as an object capable of supporting the body in a certain way, not just as the source of some particular set of retinal images. The problem is not simply one of pattern classification however complex the patterns (classification implies a finite set of responses). It includes being able to describe visual scenes; to see first a wall, then the rows of bricks; and to see a world full of objects and people with which to interact in an indefinite number of ways.

This type of flexibility is the antithesis of the making of pre-determined responses to rather stereotyped stimuli, and it exists not only in perception but in most other modes of behaviour. Philosophers have tended to identify this flexibility with free will. They were right in pointing out that certain types of mechanistic explanations were inadequate to explain these kinds of behaviour but wrong in neglecting the possibility that qualitatively different physical systems might encompass these matters. The situation in brain research today is that of having to find out what these qualitatively different mechanisms might be.

## A seeing machine

Since a physical device that could see must interpret stimulus patterns as objects on the basis of some knowledge of what objects are like, this is the point at which to start. Because the brain is of limited size the quantity of this knowledge needs to be limited but, unlike the situation in a stimulus–response machine, this need not prevent the patterns of stimuli or responses which can be dealt with from being indefinitely numerous.

A number of computer programs have been written recently which explore the problem of interpreting two-dimensional patterns (such as exist on the retina) as three-dimensional scenes containing objects. It is not without significance that in the attempts that have been made to get computers to analyse ordinary (three-dimensional) scenes that are 'looked at' by the machine via a television camera, the first operations that the machine does consist of translating patches of different shades of grey into outline shapes. This corresponds closely to what the cells that detect spots, lines and edges, that have been found by Hubel, Wiesel and others in the visual systems of animals, seem to be doing.

One of the interesting programs written to explore the next stage of analysis is that of Adolfo Guzman, of the Massachusetts Institute of Technology. Essentially his program analyses patterns which we see as line drawings of solid objects, and identifies those regions of the picture which correspond to what people

*Opposite: in order to recognize the blocks in its environment the Stanford robot (p. 178) tries to translate them into outline figures. This may seem a simple matter, but the progression from a photograph to a digitized grey scale version (top), to the boundaries of areas of constant intensity (centre), to fitted lines to give the final figure (bottom) shows it is not, since points of maximum brightness do not always correspond to the edges of objects. Many of the intermediate stages in the computation are not shown*

recognize as the surfaces making up each single object. Because of its rather surprising perspicacity it is worth examining how Guzman's program works.

First the picture is resolved into regions (areas totally enclosed by the three or more lines) and vertices (junctions between two or more lines). Each region is then labelled with a number, and each vertex with a letter. Then for each region three lists are composed and stored in the computer. Going round each region in an anti-clockwise direction lists are made of 1. each neighbouring region, 2. each vertex that is passed going round the boundary, and 3. each neighbouring region and vertex alternately. Three similar lists are then composed and stored in association with each vertex, together with the $x$ and $y$ co-ordinates (i.e. the position) of that vertex.

Working on this set of stored lists the program looks at each vertex in turn and assigns it to one of seven different classes (this is done by counting the number of lines that form it, and, from the co-ordinates of each, calculating the angles between these lines).

Next comes the important part of the program. The computer searches for regions that might be parts of the same solid body, on the basis of the types of corner that exist. For instance, if two adjacent regions meet at the kind of vertex classified as a fork then so-called 'strong links' between them are listed. These links are simply statements that the two surfaces belong together, and in the next stage they are treated as strong evidence for the final decomposition of the picture into all the separate 'solid bodies' that make it up. Various other types of vertex also give strong links between the regions, which will be regarded as strong evidence for the regions being part of the same body. The program then lists weak links, representing slightly less reliable evidence that regions should be associated.

Then the program sorts these lists of links and, on the basis of at least two strong links being needed to indicate that two regions should go together, it lists separately all those regions that should be associated as a single object. Finally mopping-up operations are

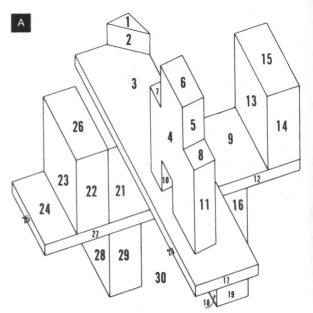

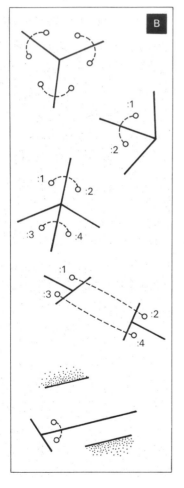

performed. One strong and one weak link are considered enough evidence to associate two regions. Then, if any single regions are associated with groupings of regions by only a single strong link, provided that the single region does not have a link with any other grouping, it too is assimilated into the grouping. The program then prints out these lists of all the regions that go to make up the separate solid bodies.

Some important points arise from this program. Firstly, although not very complicated, it will work with an infinite set of input patterns, and, except for the restrictions that they be straight-line diagrams, it has no preconceptions of the kind that are embodied in template matching devices about what patterns to expect. Thus on the stimulus side at least, this program has broken right away from the idea of the stimulus–response machine. The program does not attempt to detect object-like patterns in the line diagrams and after complicated changes to make the patterns compatible with the finite set of pre-established templates. In many ways Guzman's program is still rather limited;

for instance, it cannot describe the objects or their relationships but merely lists which regions belong together as an object.

The problem has, however, been taken further by Max Clowes at the University of Sussex. He supposes that what Guzman's program must really be doing is deploying a knowledge of the primitive geometry of three-dimensional objects. The program knows, in other words, what kinds of junction in the line diagram can arise from a particular type of corner of an object, and what kinds cannot.

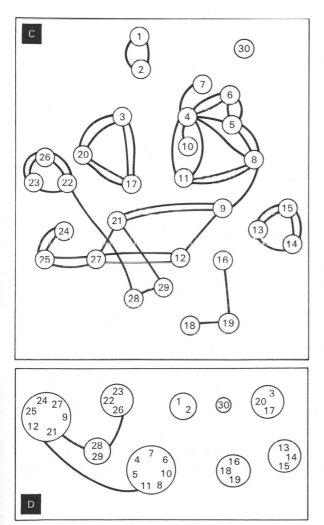

*Guzman's program on machine recognition of visual scenes works with line drawings which we immediately interpret as three-dimensional. Opposite: the program starts by labelling the regions of the scene (A); certain types of junctions between lines are then taken as evidence for regions being surfaces of the same solid, and links are listed between them, as indicated by the dotted lines (B). The program then lists regions with strong links between them, shown as lines (C). After merging regions with more than two strong links between them and then those with weaker links (D) the program finally ends up with a list of surfaces belonging together as parts of single objects (which in this case successfully coincides with the one that people would make)*

*Clowe's program considers the kinds of edge that each line drawn onto the display screen could represent, and then looks for self-consistent interpretations. In the pyramid drawing the computer has thickened those interpreted as edges joining a seen surface with an unseen one behind it, has left them alone for convex edges, and redrawn them dotted if they are considered concave. Thus this interpretation is of one tetrahedron stuck down on the background with another floating in front of it. Right: the program declares this to be an impossible solid since convex edges at one end become concave at the other, a physical impossibility allowing no self-consistent interpretation*

Clowes therefore defines two domains, the two-dimensional picture domain which is rather like the pattern on the retina, and the object, or scene domain. His program sets out to interpret the configurations of lines in the picture domain, as seen objects. (Workers in artificial intelligence have acquired a taste for acronyms and puns, with computers called such things as MANIAC, so it is not altogether a surprise that Clowes' program should have been named OB-SCENE.)

The program very deliberately and explicitly sets out the knowledge of three-dimensional plane-sided objects the computer must have not only to list which regions go together as Guzman's program does but to interpret each line and vertex as arising from possible edges and corners of object surfaces. It is therefore capable of exposing the ambiguity of line drawings, that is to say, of pointing out that simple drawings can correspond to more than one type of solid object in the scene domain. It can describe which objects are behind which other ones, it even rejects impossible figures as being capable of no self-consistent interpretation as a solid object.

Clowes's program, though it draws on Guzman's

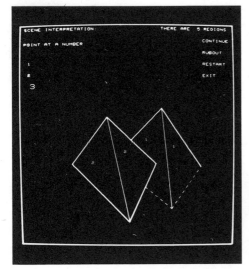

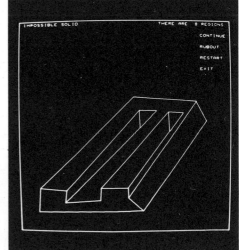

*The famous picture of Escher exploit the same failure to meet the requirements of the geometry of three-dimensional space as does the impossible object on the opposite page*

idea of using vertices to identify which surfaces belong together, has a much richer structure that begins to display what might be involved in an interpretive process of perception.

## Robots and men

At present, machines which exhibit aspects of intelligent behaviour do not begin to match the range, the incisiveness, or the richness of human ability. Nor may such relatively advanced programs as Clowes's employ methods that are similar to the ones that men use to construct within their minds the perception of three-dimensional objects from two-dimensional input patterns. What such programs do, however, is to show what general kinds of processes seem to be needed, and to suggest ways in which the problem might be tackled.

Programs such as Guzman's or Clowes's begin to show how patterns impinging on the retina can be (and must be) decomposed into their parts, and begin to demonstrate the importance of being able to describe and interpret the relationships between these parts. These faculties of decomposition, description and interpretation are prerequisites for adequate classification of objects in the scene. Since we do not respond directly to patterns in the domain of retinal images, we

*One indication from an experiment by Shepard that perception necessarily involves interpretations of line drawings as objects is that it is no more difficult to see that objects are the same, though one has been rotated around an axis through the object (B), than if the picture itself is turned round (A). The objects in (C) are not the same under any rotation*

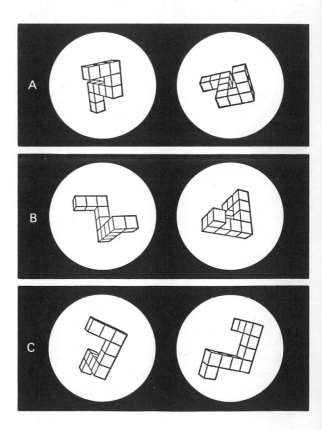

need first to decompose and interpret these patterns into things in the domain of the real world. Only then can we identify these things and act towards them appropriately.

In perception both by brains and machines we will also need to know not only how particular instances of these interpretive processes work, but also how we can switch from one to another kind of interpretation so that first we see a table, then the grain of the wood then the fact that one of the legs is not straight and needs mending. How is it that the nature of the interpretation itself imposes an appropriate form of interpretive process upon the patterns of retinal images being analysed?

In order to make interpretations of any kind the interpretive structure clearly needs to contain some knowledge of what interpretations are possible, what the world is like, what kinds of things happen and what kinds of relationships can exist. We are by no means sure what the extent of this knowledge needs to be, but the concept corresponds to Craik's idea of the model which reflects the workings of the world, to Chomsky's notion of competence, or to Piaget's postulates of the logical concepts which each child seems to grasp. The model is however not just knowledge, but includes the idea of mechanism. It has a metaphorical handle which can be cranked to make this internal representation actually work to produce predictions, or behaviour, or perception.

The problem as it seems today of understanding natural intelligence, and of creating artificial intelligence is centred upon the problems of what knowledge needs to be embodied in such models, how items should be arranged to represent effectively the world with which we interact, and how the structure of knowledge enables behaviour to be performed. This matter is central to fields other than perception. Problem-solving, question-answering, game-playing and the construction of robots that can interact sensibly with a natural environment all demand the discovery of effective representational systems.

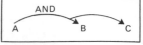

B names a class of which A is a subclass

A, B and C form a conjunctive set

*A part of Ross Quillian's illustration of his program for semantically organized memory. Right: some of the links that can be set between words. Below: the networks built up from dictionary definitions of the word 'plant' so that various kinds of association can be interpreted to have particular meanings*

B modifies A

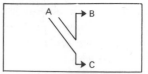

A, B and C form a disjunctive set

B, a subject, is related to C, an object, in the manner specified by A, the relation. Either the link to B or to C may be omitted, which implies that A's normal subject or object is to be assumed.

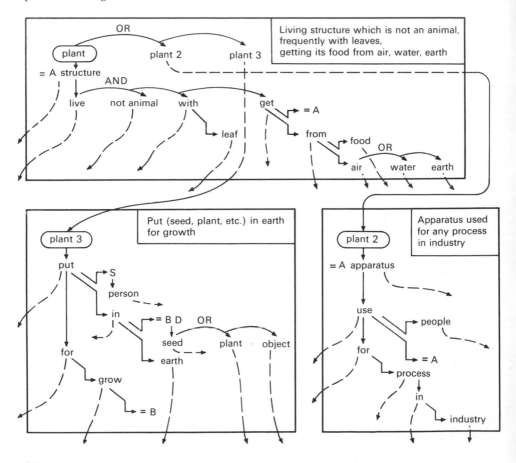

## The structure of knowledge

A major aspect of the problem of representing knowledge was raised at the end of Chapter 8, in the discussion of human memory. Just as in human memory knowledge has to be organized in structures that reflect the relationships of objects in the world, so too the knowledge that we would give to a computer with which we wish to converse must have these characteristics.

One such program for question-answering has been written by Ross Quillian, and in it semantic relationships are stored in a manner not unlike that which Chomsky has supposed must constitute the deep structure of sentences. The type of structure used in the program is shown opposite. Essentially it consists of words related to other words by different kinds of link. For instance, one type of link signifies 'is a member of the class', in the sense that 'table' is a member of the class 'furniture'. Not every type of relationship has a special link: some relationships are symbolized by words, because in natural language very many things can be considered as mediating relationships. Each word is linked to its own cluster of words (properties) which together go to make up its definition. Of course each of the words appearing in the definition (of the kind that is fed to the computer) is also attached to its own cluster, so that the structure soon becomes complex and interconnected.

With the ability to make such structures the computer can be told things, and it interprets what it is told by storing new words with appropriate links between them. Thus it would interpret the word 'is' in 'A table is furniture' as meaning that it has to set the link meaning 'is a member of the class' between 'table' and 'furniture'. When answering questions it re-interprets links to form English sentences. The sort of English it produces is what Quillian describes as in the 'Me Tarzan, you Jane' style but nevertheless passage around such structures is very much like pursuing an idea.

One type of question the program can be asked is to relate two words that it has stored. It responds to this by searching the structure, spreading out from each word until it finds a point at which pathways from each meet, and it then translates these pathways into sentences. A typical example was: relate 'earth' and 'live'. The program found that the first word that was common to the pathways of links spreading out from each of these was 'animal', and it then produced the sentences: 1. 'Earth is planet of animal', 2. 'To live is to have existence as animal'.

As in Guzman's program, the behaviour is as yet limited, but nevertheless rather surprisingly thoughtful. In other words, relatively complex behaviour emerges from certain postulates about the nature of memory, when these are translated into a particular representation or model.

At present, workers in artificial intelligence are actively experimenting with the structure of knowledge and its representation. When it actually comes to writing computer programs that learn one perceives that it is all too easy simply to store information or form new connections, and we see very clearly that in getting a computer to do that we have not shown anything very profound or satisfying about the nature of learning. In order to be able to talk about what learning consists of we have instead to be able to specify how relevant aspects of the world are represented, what significance is assigned to these various aspects, and how the knowledge is organized in such a way that we can, as it were, compute over it to solve problems. In other words, if we can understand some of the general properties of representational systems we may, for instance, be able to understand the process of learning not as altering some parameter, or changing the probability of some response, but as acquiring successively more effective representations to cope with the situations we are faced with.

# THE BRAIN AND ITS FUTURE

I have tried to give the flavour of what seems to its practitioners in neurophysiology, psychology, linguistics and artificial intelligence, to be an unfolding development of brain research. It is quite probable that future recognition of basic principles, as yet unconceived, may make some of what has gone before seem obsolete. At present we may fail to apprehend these principles, for the same reason that for centuries man failed to apprehend Newton's first law of motion. In some way our own minds, which we have set out to understand, may not be constructed to discern immediately important facts or draw right conclusions.

Nevertheless, since Descartes' first ideas about the mechanism of behaviour, several conceptual revolutions have swept away fallacies. Technological advance has allowed us to examine the brain down to a scale of thousandths of a second of time, and millionths of a centimetre of distance. Technology has given us computers in which we can create altogether new minds. Already we have discovered facts and reached understandings which establish the scientific study of brain mechanisms and mind on very firm ground. There is also good reason to believe that the newer ideas about the nature of representation in the brain may have very far-reaching significance.

There are, however, problems of fundamental interest and importance which we are little nearer to understanding now than two thousand years ago. In the consideration of man's mind what, for instance, could seem more central but less understood than consciousness?

## Consciousness and the unconscious

Consciousness, although it may also be other things, seems to be the faculty for observation of and commentary upon at least some of our own higher-order mental processes. Whether as well as commentator the conscious self has any role as director may be a meaningless question, since the same set of mental processes that takes place also offers the commentary upon itself. It may be that the necessity for perceptual processes to include interpretation and re-interpretation, and for processes of understanding and knowledge to grow and become reorganized, requires a sort of internal discussion at the highest logical level. Maybe this internal discussion is consciousness. Though this is mere speculation, it seems possible that a machine with the same abilities to perceive and think as we do, would need to indulge in the same kind of internal discussion, and that this too would amount to consciousness. Maybe consciousness is due to the mind having a representation of itself, and this again might not be impossible to embody in a computer.

What seems clear is that we have no consciousness of, or private access to, many lower brain processes. We have no internal means of inspecting patterns on our retina for instance; they are transformed at each stage of the analysis and interpretation process. We have no internal view of the organization of motor networks that allow us to ride a bicycle. In just the same way the driver of a car, as he sits in the driving seat, has no way of inspecting the workings of the steering linkage. Nor does he need to. He is more concerned with steering than almost anything else as he drives, but whether the car's steering box has a rack and pinion, or worm and wheel gear is of no immediate interest to him.

Most of the processes of our brains take place automatically, and we have neither the need nor the ability

*Automatic transmission frees the driver for other things; he is unconscious of what is going on in the gear box. Similarly, many mental processes occur automatically, and without our being aware of them*

to inspect them directly. If we had to think actively and consciously about such things as which muscles to move in order to sign our name we would never have time to do anything else. In 1899 the authors of one of the earliest psychological papers on the learning of skills concluded that acquisition was the process of making perceptual and motor processes automatic, so that the mind could be freed for more important matters. 'There is no freedom but through automatism,' they remarked.

Freud, when he claimed that the greater part of mental activity was unconscious was absolutely right. Where he seems wrong was in attributing unconsciousness to wishes and desires rather than to the automatic machinery of the brain. Wishes and desires are exactly the kind of things that are available for commentary, and the success of psychoanalysis depends upon such commentaries being carried on in a protracted way in the expensive presence of an analyst.

## Experiment and theory

Apart from Freud's apparent misuse of the term, consciousness has been viewed in two ways by brain researchers. Initially psychologists saw it as a means for inspecting the workings of the mind, and tried to train themselves in introspection. Largely because they were trying to inspect the automatic processes which are by nature unconscious they failed. In the meantime, Helmholtz, Sherrington and Pavlov, followed by an army of experimental psychologists who doubted the value of introspection, measured behaviour from which the internal workings of some parts of the nervous system could be inferred. The most detailed explanations of behaviour that we have today are of precisely those mechanisms which are unconscious and automatic.

At the same time as the excitement of success in beginning to be able to explain behaviour in terms of the nervous system there has been a gradual realization that the aspects of the brain that were profitably being dealt with were those of lower levels. We have learned something about the processing of sensory signals, but rather less about perception, about speaking but not much about saying something, about hearing but not about understanding. It may be, however, as Chomsky implies, that the time has come for a new informed kind of introspection in brain research; consulting our own intuitions not about matters which are by nature unconscious, but about what it is that we know about the world, and about matters from which we can deduce our competence for thought, speech and action.

## The future

One neurophysiologist friend of mine was fond of saying that the best thing about his work was that it had no possible practical applications. In a climate where scientific knowledge is often turned to evil account, through good intentions or bad, maybe the best status for any research is as a very academic pursuit. Despite this there has been, and there continues to be, some very useful spin-off. Perhaps most important, the mere fact of trying to understand brain and mind in objective terms has meant that we now treat such matters as mental illness much more sympathetically than ever before. More immediately, physiological psychology gives a rationale for the action of drugs used in psychiatry, and certainly our understanding in this area will continue to grow with the result that we will be better able to treat the neurologically and mentally ill. The fruits of applied psychology have started to appear all around us in forms which range from the layout of cockpits in aircraft and space capsules, to the way in which letters are sorted in the Post Office. Education too has benefited from psychology, both directly and because of the atmosphere of general enlightenment.

Though it would be possible to try and predict in detail the developments of the next ten years, such attempts at prophecy are largely idle.

The potential importance of extensions of some of

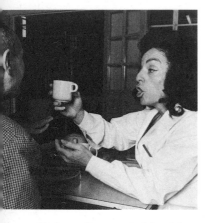

*Understandings acquired from laboratory work with animals can be applied to psychiatric problems. Here Dr I. Kassorla is using behaviour therapy based on a reinforcement principle to treat a patient who was described as 'the sickest man in a British mental institution'. Dr Kassorla had some success in getting this patient, who had been silent for 39 years, to talk and behave more normally*

the research I have described is so great, however, that we must consider the more distant future. It seems essential that we should have thought sufficiently so that if fundamental choices about the nature of society, the extent to which we should allow machines to do our intellectual as well as physical work, and suchlike are to be made, they should be made carefully and deliberately. There is certainly little cause for alarm at present; our understanding of too many fundamental problems is too meagre. Nevertheless, I offer the rest of this book not as prediction but as possibility. Other possibilities exist, and no doubt readers will make their own extrapolation into the future.

One implication of being able to understand fundamental properties of the brain such as memory, perception, language and so on, is that we will be able to program these properties in computers. Possibly we will need to program these processes before we can understand how they are achieved in the human brain. However it comes about though, the understanding of such processes as human thought brings with it the possibility of being able to program a computer to perform better than ourselves.

The history of human invention has been that of improving upon the abilities with which we were born. Far from taking the view that man is already a perfect creation, inventors have always thought of doing better. Mechanical transport allows us to travel more efficiently, cranes allow heavier weights to be lifted, telescopes allow us to see further and so on. There does not seem to be any limit to intelligence that can be discerned at present and therefore we may be able to design computers that can think better than us. Clearly if such machines were more intelligent than ourselves, then these too would be capable of designing machines more intelligent than themselves.

## A psychologically controlled world

The vision of the future that follows from understanding the human mind is therefore probably not that of George Orwell's *1984* in which the techniques of

*Above: the cockpits of aircraft ought to be carefully designed to display information so that it will be both noticed and understood, a very difficult task in view of the quantity of information and limited visual area. Below: a classic example of how not to present information, seeming almost to have been designed to encourage meter readers to make mistakes*

*The spectre of complete control not only over behaviour, but also over thoughts was created with great power by George Orwell. As our understanding of psychology increases the world of '1984' may come closer*

brainwashing and psychological deception are used to subjugate man. The cost of keeping complete watch on many individuals would be very great, and the idea that any particular individual can ever be totally understood is probably a paranoid fear. Perhaps Orwell's vision should not be dismissed, though. Effective psychological manipulation already takes place with only the most primitive of operational understandings. Advertising and the persuasive techniques of marketing are a continuous reminder of this. Even more disturbing may be the insidious growth of Orwellian *doublethink*: in Britain, the place from which unemployment pay is drawn now bears a sign saying 'Department of Employment and Productivity', and the ruthless slaughter occasioned by defence is even more horrific than what used to be produced by war.

The *Brave New World* of Aldous Huxley is another possibility. There the spectre is of test-tube babies, infantile conditioning, the completely engineered environment and the meaninglessness of drug-induced pleasure. This too is not without signs of coming to pass. Marijuana seems a very good first step towards *soma*, the panacea of *Brave New World* which induces pleasure, synthetic togetherness and catharsis but no hangover. No doubt as we understand the brain mechanisms of emotional states and their transmitter substances better we will be able to develop drugs yet closer to the ideal.

More benign, though less likely, is Skinner's *Walden Two*, a Utopian experimental community. In this book Skinner paints a picture of unrelieved optimism, apparently the only modern writer about the future to do so. In *Walden Two*, ennui, poverty, competitiveness and the other ills of society are eliminated, and replaced by communal responsibility, affection, joy in work, excellence in the creative arts and unalloyed happiness. 'Splendid,' one thinks, 'I'll join immediately.' But how is it done? Throughout the book Skinner drops broader and broader hints as to the way in which this marvellous society comes to pass, but not until near the end is the secret fully revealed. Reinforcement theory is the answer; the power of positive reinforcement can make men whole and happy, as well as shaping their behaviour into acceptable patterns. 'What is love', asks the founder of the Walden Two community 'except another name for the use of positive reinforcement?'

Unlike Orwell and Huxley, Skinner is a professional psychologist so maybe his account is the more authoritative. Could a behaviourally engineered future be possible in which our performance on carefully selected schedules of reinforcement was made both socially beneficial and personally satisfying? Skinner's book has been described as stunning in its naïveté. Fortunately or unfortunately positive reinforcement schedules, excellent though they are for some types of animal training, have not been shown to provide a means for the infinite moulding of either animal or human behaviour.

In the book, too, Skinner's protagonist has hard things to say about college professors. Set beside putting reinforcement theory to work in an experimental community even such a scientific achievement as 'the splitting of the atom pales into insignificance'. Nevertheless, the community of Walden Two is still unfounded, and the use of reinforcement theory by society is exhibited chiefly in the distribution of positive and negative reinforcements (foreign aid and bombs) in attempts to shape the behaviour of nations into the embrace of *doublethink* peace and freedom.

## The new men

None of these books has quite the same sort of power or plausibility as has Olaf Stapledon's *Last and First Men*. Here after cycles of near self-extinction man conceives, and finally begins to achieve, the task of improvement of the human race. He does so, according to Stapledon, in the end by genetic engineering, making new biological men out of biological units.

The nature of the brain as a means of representing its environment and itself in order to be able to operate

*Marijuana: perhaps the first step towards Huxley's imagined drug 'soma' which kept the 'Brave New World' happy and (mostly) in one piece*

independently, and not simply respond to stimuli, unlike older mechanical conceptions asserts the possibility of free will. Also, in that the representationally based mechanisms of the brain are capable of creativeness, maybe they are also capable of progressive self improvement without genetic engineering.

In any case, although Stapledon's aspiration seems a noble one, it now seems less likely that we shall achieve it by biological means. It is, however, possible that we could program computers to be not only more intelligent, but in other ways better than ourselves; kinder, more loyal, unselfish, without deceit and, in fact, more perfectly the possessor of man's most valued qualities than any men have yet been able to be. Our mechanical progeny could be freed of the petty encumbrances of aggression, self-love, and suspiciousness which we inherit from our animal past, when those traits may have been essential for survival. If we are to survive today it seems, on the contrary, essential that we be freed of them; and how else but by creating a new type of man?

The fact that our successors would be made not of biological materials but of physical ones may seem repugnant. Yet it is mere prejudice that repels us. Successors who could have the abilities and traits which we want to give them, while at the same time being better than we are, might be very much more worthy than the offspring whom we at present bring into the world and on whom we confer the same unpleasant characteristics that we ourselves possess.

Furthermore, freedom from the biological ball and chain would allow the new beings freedoms hitherto only dreamed of or imagined as the most improbable fantasy. Since the nature of the individual would be that of a logical organization, a program which merely had to inhabit a computer in order to actualize itself, it could be transmitted through space with no more difficulty than a television programme, and at the speed of light, to some suitable recipient machine. Furthermore, since the actual hardware of the machine would be replaceable, without destroying the pro-

gram that specifies its interconnections, an individual would be effectively immortal, until it chose to replace itself with a better version. Space travel, between solar systems which for reasons of mere distance seem impossible for biological man, immediately begins to seem plausible.

The new individuals would be capable of being directly connected to stores of the accumulated knowledge of all previous civilization. Perhaps even more importantly, individuals would either be capable of operating separately, or of directly interconnecting with others, and perhaps in this way achieving states to which biological man has aspired, but which he has never reached.

It seems possible that man as we know him will ultimately be superseded, though the new race would certainly be kinder and more considerate to us than we would be to another intelligent species, or are now to members of our own species. It seems likely, though, that we will die out in any case; victims either of our own profligacy, or of bombs, nerve gas or one of the several other instruments of suicide in the armoury of overkill.

Regretfully, I have to report that in the event of any such occurrence within the next few years we will not have had time to understand the principles of mental organization sufficiently to build a self-improving and intelligent successor who would be capable of surviving the cataclysm.

*One result of understanding the brain may be that we will be able to improve on it. Hal, the space ship computer in the science-fiction film '2001', was so capable that it was not clear why human astronauts were needed on the voyage*

# GLOSSARY

**artificial intelligence**: a name given to attempts to produce mental processes in computers, and make machines behave intelligently.

**axon**: the long fibre which transmits neural messages away from the neurone cell body.

**brain lesions**: damage to or removal of parts of the brain. They may be performed so that changes in behaviour may be observed.

**control systems**: a system which controls particular events usually with reference to some internalized model, and to measurements of its own activity.

**classical conditioning**: a form of learning discovered by Pavlov in which a stimulus repeatedly occurring before some event of importance to the animal comes to acquire predictive significance.

**cortex**: the outside covering ($1\cdot5$-3 mm. thick) of the brain containing mostly neurone bodies and dendrites rather than axon tracts.

**dendrites**: structures continuous with the bodies of neurones which form surfaces upon which synapses occur and via which information is received from other cells.

**electrode**: an electrically-conducting probe or piece of metal via which electrical signals from nerves can be recorded or electrical stimulation delivered.

**experimental psychology**: the investigation of behaviour in animals and men and the attempt to understand the logical structure of brain mechanisms responsible for behaviour.

**grammar**: a system of rules which is capable of generating sentences which are judged by a native speaker of a language to be correct.

**hormones**: chemical messengers carried in the blood.

**ions**: electric charge-carrying fragments of dissolved molecules.

**learning**: the acquisition or reorganization of information in the brain of an individual as a result of his experience, in a way that may subsequently affect his performance.

**linguistics**: the scientific study of language, and particularly the investigation and formal specification of rules and relationships underlying linguistic utterance.

**motivation**: the energization and purposeful direction of behaviour towards certain goals.

**motor nerve**: structure conveying impulses from brain or spinal cord to the muscles.

**nerve impulse**: the stereotyped unit of a neural message that travels along an axon.

**neurones**: nerve cells, units of which the nervous system is composed.

**neurophysiology**: physiological investigation of nervous tissue, nowadays largely devoted to understanding the electrical activity of the brain and interactions between nerve cells.

**perception**: the interpretation of information from receptors as objects and events.

**post-synaptic potentials**: voltage changes of graded size initiated by the arrival of transmitter substances on the post-synaptic membrane, and carrying neural information along dendrites.

**program**: the set of instructions which comprise the logical structure of operations to be performed by a computer.

**reflex**: a simple unit of behaviour involving response to a stimulus, and mediated supposedly by a chain of neuronal interconnections (reflex arc).

**reinforcement**: event that results in learning, usually now taken to mean a reward or punishment.

**retina**: the neural tissue at the back of the eye containing light-sensitive receptors and several other layers of neurones.

**sensory nerve**: structure conveying impulses from a sense organ to the spinal cord and/or brain.

**spinal cord**: the tube–like extension of the brain within the backbone.

**stimulation of the brain**: (a) electrical stimulation in the form of small alternating or intermittent currents passed through an electrode, or (b) chemical stimulation in the form of a substance injected via a small tube.

**stimulus-response theory**: the idea that behaviour is based on the reflex and that the brain acts to connect responses to stimuli present at the time of the behaviour.

**synapse**: a junction between neurones, and the point at which information can pass between neurones.

**threshold of nerve**: the voltage that has to be achieved before a nerve impulse occurs.

**transmitter substances**: chemicals released at synapses by impulses; they produce post-synaptic potentials and thereby carry information between neurones.

# SELECTED BIBLIOGRAPHY

## 1 BRAIN RESEARCH

A good general introduction is D. E. Wooldridge's *The Machinery of the Brain* (New York 1963). K. J. W. Craik's discussion of thought is in *The Nature of Explanation* (Cambridge 1943). For arguments about whether mind has a physical basis: A. M. Turing, 'Computing machinery and intelligence' in *Mind, 59* (1950) 433–60 and N. S. Sutherland, 'Is the brain a physical system?' in R. Borger and F. Cioffi (Eds.), *Explanation in the Behavioural Sciences* (Cambridge 1970) 97–122. E. Elcock and A. Murray's program to play Go Moku is described in 'Experiments with a learning component in a Go Moku playing program' in N. Collins and D. Michie (Eds.), *Machine Intelligence, 1* (Edinburgh 1967) 87–103.

## 2 NEURONES

One of the best texts on neurophysiology is T. Ruch, H. Patton, J. Woodbury and A. Towe, *Neurophysiology* (Philadelphia 1965). A historical account can be found in M. A. B. Brazier, 'The historical development of neurophysiology' in *The Handbook of Physiology*, Section 1, Vol 1 (American Physiological Society 1959) 1–58 or, for selections from original sources, E. Clarke and C. O'Malley, *The Human Brain and Spinal Cord* (Berkeley 1968). H. Helmholtz is best introduced by his *Popular Scientific Lectures* (New York 1962). Pioneers of neuronal recording have written lucidly on the subject, the best book being B. Katz, *Nerve muscle and synapse* (New York 1966). See also A. L. Hodgkin, *The Conduction of the Nervous Impulse* (Liverpool 1967) and J. C. Eccles, *The Physiology of Nerve Cells* (Baltimore 1957).

## 3 STRUCTURE AND FUNCTION

An introduction to the study of fossil man is W. E. Le Gros Clark's, *History of the Primates* (London 1954, Chicago 1966). The influence of Gall and phrenology is assessed by E. Boring in *A History of Experimental Psychology* (New York 1950). Accounts of brain anatomy are given in many textbooks, e.g. R. Thompson, *Foundations of Physiological Psychology* (New York 1967). One of the most interesting books on neuro-anatomy is D. A. Sholl, *The Organization of the Cerebral Cortex* (London 1956). Penfield's work is described in W. Penfield and T. Rasmussen, *The Cerebral Cortex of Man* (New York 1957).

## 4 INFORMATION

E. D. Adrian described his work in *The Basis of Sensation* (Boston 1928). For more recent accounts of sensory systems see H. Davis, 'Some principles of sensory receptor action' in *Physiological Review, 41* (1961) 391–416. C. Sherrington's most important work is *The Integrative Action of the Nervous System* (Yale 1906), now in paperback. An excellent account of the significance of Sherrington's research is given by P. A. Merton in 'The central nervous system', Chapter 14 of F. Winton and L. Bayliss's *Human Physiology* (London, 5th ed. 1962).

## 5 THE DETECTION OF PATTERN

A book which deals with how neurones act in networks is G. A. Horridge's *Interneurons* (San Francisco 1968). Some excellent books have been written on vision; still the best is H. Helmholtz, *Treatise on Physiological Optics* (English translation, New York 1962). M. H. Pirenne, *Vision and the Eye* (London 1948) is a good introduction, and a very worthwhile up-to-date book is T. Cornsweet's *Visual Perception* (New York 1970). G. Wald compares 'Eye and Camera' in *Scientific American* August 1950. Cells of the retina have all been recorded from by F. S. Werblin and J. E. Dowling, 'Organization of the retina of the mudpuppy: II Intracellular recording' in *Journal of Neurophysiology, 32* (1969) 339–55. Movement-detecting cells were described by H. B. Barlow and W. R. Levick, 'The mechanism of directionally sensitive units in the rabbit's retina' in *Journal of Physiology, 178* (1965) 477–504. Typical colour-sensitive neurones have been described by R. L. de Valois, 'Behavioural and electrophysiological studies of primate vision' in *Contributions to*

Sensory Physiology Vol 1 (New York 1965). D. H. Hubel and T. N. Wiesel's well-known discoveries were first presented in 'Receptive fields of single neurones in the cat's striate cortex' in Journal of Physiology, 148 (1959) 574–91. For K. Dunker's experiment see W. Ellis (Ed.) Source book of Gestalt Psychology (London 1938) 161–72. Based partly on Hubel & Wiesel's work is N. S. Sutherland's 'Outline of a theory of visual pattern recognition in animals and man' in Proceedings of the Royal Society B, 171 (1968) 297–317.

## 6 SEEING IS BELIEVING

A good introduction to the psychology of visual perception is R. L. Gregory's Eye and Brain (London and New York 1966), and a useful collection of psychological experiments is R. N. Haber's Contemporary Theory and Research in Visual Perception (New York 1968). K. Koffka's book is Principles of Gestalt Psychology (London and New York 1935). L. Wittgenstein discusses perception in Philosophical Investigations (Oxford 1958). A. Holway's and E. Boring's experiment is described in 'Determinants of apparent visual size with distance variant' in American Journal of Psychology, 51 (1941) 21–37. Depth cues are discussed by, for example, W. Ittleson, Visual space perception (New York 1960). Perception of space is also discussed by J. J. Gibson in The Perception of the Visual World (Boston 1950). For B. Julesz's work see 'Binocular perception without familiarity cues' in Science, 145 (1964) 356–62. E. H. Gombrich's book Art and Illusion was published in London in 1960. M. H. Pirenne's Optics, Painting and Photography (Cambridge 1970), is also worthwhile.

## 7 BEHAVIOUR WITH A PURPOSE

C. Darwin's Origin of Species was first published in 1859 and has been much reprinted. N. Wiener's book Cybernetics (New York 1948) was an important milestone. The application of control theory to psychological problems is well introduced by D. Mcfarland in Feedback Mechanisms in Animal Behaviour (New York 1971). C. L. Hull's theory was presented (amongst other places) in Essentials of Behaviour (Yale 1951). The type of analysis of motivation described here was presented by K. Oatley in 'Brain mechanisms and motivation' in Nature, 225 (1970) 797–801, but see P. Teitelbaum 'The biology of drive' in The Neurosciences, Eds. G. Quarton, T. Melnechuk and F. Schmitt (New York 1967), 557–67, for a quite different view. The subject of sleep is well introduced

by W. B. Webb in Sleep, an Experimental Approach (London and New York 1968). For the role of timing in behaviour see K. Oatley and B. C. Goodwin 'The explanation and investigation of biological rhythms' in W. P. Colquhoun (Ed.) Biological Rhythms and Human Performance (New York 1971) 1–38. W. R. Hess describes his work in Diencephalon, Autonomic and Extrapyramidal Functions (New York 1954). Experiments on electrical stimulation are referenced and discussed in all Physiological Psychology texts including Thompson op.cit. or P. Milner Physiological Psychology (New York 1970). The innateness of electrically-stimulated behaviour was shown by W. W. Roberts and E. H. Bergquist, 'Attack elicited by hypothalamic stimulation in cats raised in social isolation' in Journal of Comparative Physiological Psychology, 66 (1968) 590–8.

## 8 LEARNING AND MEMORY

A standard work on learning is G. Kimble's revision of Hilgard and Marquis, Conditioning and Learning (London 1961). I. P. Pavlov described his work in Conditioned Reflexes (New York 1960). J. B. Watson's book Behaviourism was first published in Chicago in 1924 and is now a paperback. A good introduction to Skinner's work is in B. F. Skinner, Cumulative Record (New York 1961). A sympathetic but critical appraisal of Skinner's work is given by R. A. Boakes and M. S. Halliday, 'The Skinnerian analysis of behaviour' in Borger and Cioffi (Eds.) op.cit. 345–74. Ability of pigeons to avoid shock by running was shown by E. Macphail, 'Avoidance responding in pigeons' in Journal of the Experimental Analysis of Behavior, 11 (1968) 629–52, and the special mechanism of alimentary learning is discussed by J. Garcia and F. Ervin, 'Gustatory visceral and telereceptor cutaneous conditioning – adaptation in external and internal milieus' in Communications in Behavioural Biology, Part A 1, 389–415 (1968). K. Lashley's work was best described by himself: Brain mechanisms and Intelligence (New York 1963). An up-to-date treatment of discrimination learning is by N. S. Sutherland and N. T. Mackintosh, Mechanisms of Animal Discrimination Learning (New York 1971). The idea of a biochemical basis of memory is reviewed by D. A. Booth, 'Vertebrate brain RNA and memory retention, in Psychological Bulletin 68 (1967) 149–77. Human memory is discussed by U. Neisser in Cognitive Psychology (New York 1967) and by D. Norman in Memory and Attention (New York 1969). Differences between short and long term memory have been investigated by A. D. Baddeley, for example: 'Effects of acoustic and semantic similarity on short-term paired associate learning' in *British Journal of Psychology 61* (1970) 335–43. F. C. Bartlett described his work in *Remembering* (Cambridge 1932).

## 9 LANGUAGE AND THOUGHT

A recent account of D. Premack's attempt to teach the ape Sarah elements of language is in 'Language in chimpanzee?' in *Science 172* (1971) 808–22. J. Lyons' *Introduction to Theoretical Linguistics* (Cambridge 1968) is very good, as is his *Chomsky* (London 1970, New York 1971). B. F. Skinner's *Verbal Behaviour* (New York 1957) was reviewed by N. Chomsky in *Language*, *35* (1959) 26–58. The most easily approached of Chomsky's books is *Language and Mind* (New York 1968), but *Aspects of the Theory of Syntax* (Cambridge, Mass. 1965) is the definitive work. Psycholinguistics is introduced by G. A. Miller, 'Some preliminaries to psycholinguistics' in *American Psychologist*, *20* (1965) 15–20. R. Brown's work on children's grammar is described in his collected papers entitled *Psycholinguistics* (Chicago 1970). J. Piaget's writing is so extensive that it is perhaps best approached via J. H. Flavell, *The Developmental Psychology of Jean Piaget* (Princeton 1963). The organization of logical thought is lucidly discussed by M. Wertheimer, *Productive Thinking* (New York 1945, London 1961). H. Jenkins' and W. Ward's experiments are in 'Judgements of contingency between responses and outcomes' in *Psychological Monographs*, *79*, whole No. 594 (1965). A stimulating analysis of the nature of scientific understanding is by T. Kuhn *The Structure of Scientific Revolutions* (Chicago 1962).

## 10 ARTIFICIAL BRAINS

The best introduction to artificial intelligence is E. Feigenbaum and J. Feldman (Eds.), *Computers and Thought* (New York 1963), and the chapters by Minsky in M. Minsky (Ed.) *Semantic Information Processing* (Cambridge, Mass. 1968). The problem of seeing as tackled by work with the Stanford robot is in C. R. Brice and C. L. Fennema's 'Scene analysis using regions' in *Artificial Intelligence 1* (1970) 205–26. A. Guzman describes his program in 'Decomposition of a visual scene into three-dimensional bodies' in A. Grasselli (Ed.), *Automatic Interpretation and Classification of Images* (New York 1969) 243–76. M. Clowes' work is 'On seeing things' in *Artificial Intelligence*, *2* (1971) 79–116. R. Quillian describes his research in 'Semantic memory' which is pp. 216–70 of M. Minsky (Ed.), *op.cit.*

## 11 THE BRAIN AND ITS FUTURE

S. Freud's work is easily approached via *Psychopathology of Everday Life*, first published in 1914 and now in paperback. An early paper on skills as automatic behaviour was W. Bryan and W. Harter's 'Studies in telegraphic language' in *Psychological Review*, *6* (1899) 345–75. The novels mentioned were G. Orwell, *1984*, A. Huxley, *Brave New World*, and O. Stapledon's *Last and First Men*, all published in paperback by Penguin; and B. F. Skinner's *Walden Two*, a Macmillan paperback. A look into the future of computers was given by N. S. Sutherland in 'Machines like men' in *Science Journal, 4* (1968) 44–8.

# LIST AND SOURCES OF ILLUSTRATIONS

# INDEX  *The numbers in italics refer to illustrations*